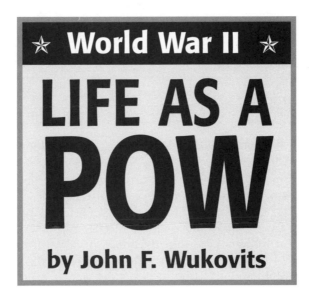

World War II

LIFE AS A POW

by John F. Wukovits

Lucent Books, P.O. Box 289011, San Diego, CA 92198-9011

Titles in The American War Library series include:

World War II
Hitler and the Nazis
Kamikazes
Leaders and Generals
Life as a POW
Life of an American Soldier in
  Europe
Strategic Battles in Europe
Strategic Battles in the Pacific
The War at Home
Weapons of War

The Civil War
Leaders of the North and South
Life Among the Soldiers and
  Cavalry
Lincoln and the Abolition of
  Slavery
Strategic Battles
Weapons of War

Dedicated to John William Mahoney
World War II Prisoner and Uncle Extraordinaire

Library of Congress Cataloging-in-Publication Data

Wukovits, John F., 1944–
    Life as a POW / John F. Wukovits.
        p.   cm.—(American war library)
    Includes bibliographical references and index.
    Summary: Describes what it was like to be an American prisoner
of war held by the Germans or Japanese during World War II,
discussing the physical conditions, emotional turmoil, and difficult
transition to freedom after harsh imprisonment.
    ISBN 1-56006-665-2 (lib. bdg. : alk. paper)
    1. World War, 1939–1945—Prisoners and prisons Juvenile
literature. 2. Prisoners of war—United States—History—20th
century Juvenile literature. [1. World War, 1939–1945—Prisoners
and prisons. 2. Prisoners of war—History—20th century.]
I. Title. II. Title: Life as a prisoner of war. III. Series: American
war library series.
D805.A2W85   2000
940.54'72'092273—dc21   99-37695
                                                                         CIP

Copyright 2000 by Lucent Books, Inc.
P.O. Box 289011, San Diego, California 92198-9011

Printed in the U.S.A.

☆ Contents ☆

A Nation Forged by War

The United States, like many nations, was forged and defined by war. Despite Benjamin Franklin's opinion that "There never was a good war or a bad peace," the United States owes its very existence to the War of Independence, one to which Franklin wholeheartedly subscribed. The country forged by war in 1776 was tempered and made stronger by the Civil War in the 1860s.

The Texas Revolution, the Mexican-American War, and the Spanish-American War expanded the country's borders and gave it overseas possessions. These wars made the United States a world power, but this status came with a price, as the nation became a key but reluctant player in both World War I and World War II.

Each successive war further defined the country's role on the world stage. Following World War II, U.S. foreign policy redefined itself to focus on the role of defender, not only of the freedom of its own citizens, but also of the freedom of people everywhere. During the cold war that followed World War II until the collapse of the Soviet Union, defending the world meant fighting communism. This goal, manifested in the Korean and Vietnam conflicts, proved elusive, and soured the American public on its achievability. As the United States emerged as the world's sole superpower, American foreign policy has been guided less by national interest and more on protecting international human rights. But as involvement in Somalia and Kosovo prove, this goal has been equally elusive.

As a result, the country's view of itself changed. Bolstered by victories in World Wars I and II, Americans first relished the role of protector. But, as war followed war in a seemingly endless procession, Americans began to doubt their leaders, their motives, and themselves. The Vietnam War especially caused people to question the validity of sending its young people to die in places where they were not particularly wanted and for people who did not seem especially grateful.

While the most obvious changes brought about by America's wars have been geopolitical in nature, many other aspects of society have been touched. War often does not bring about change directly, but acts instead like the catalyst in a chemical reaction, accelerating changes already in progress.

Some of these changes have been societal. The role of women in the United States had been slowly changing, but World War II put thousands into the workforce and into uniform. They might have gone back to being housewives after the war, but equality, once experienced, would not be forgotten.

Likewise, wars have accelerated technological change. The necessity for faster airplanes and a more destructive bomb led to the development of jet planes and nuclear energy. Artificial fibers developed for parachutes in the 1940s were used in the clothing of the 1950s.

Lucent Books' American War Library covers key wars in the development of the nation. Each war is covered in several volumes, to allow for more detail, context, and to provide volumes on often neglected subjects, such as the kamikazes of World War II, or weapons used in the Civil War. As with all Lucent Books, notes, annotated bibliographies, and appendixes such as glossaries give students a launching point for further research. In addition, sidebars and archival photographs enhance the text. Together, each volume in The American War Library will aid students in understanding how America's wars have shaped and changed its politics, economics, and society.

"I Just Tried to Forget Everything"

In early April 1999 three American soldiers—Andrew A. Ramirez, Christopher J. Stone, and Steven M. Gonzales—were taken prisoner by Yugoslav forces in Kosovo. Within one day images of the trio, showing obvious signs of beatings, appeared on television broadcasts around the world. In the United States stunned citizens, shocked at the brutal treatment of fellow countrymen, clamored for their immediate release. President Bill Clinton threatened increased military action should the three remain in custody, and congressional leaders called for swift retaliation.

"It gives [the war] a face, doesn't it?"[1] said foreign policy scholar Stephen Hess. He added that the media and the nation needed such a powerful image to add drama to a situation from which many Americans felt remote.

Eighteen years earlier, on January 20, 1981, fifty-two American men and women, held hostage for 444 days in Iran by revolutionary forces of the Muslim religious leader Ayatollah Ruhollah Khomeini, were finally set free and sent to the United States. A grateful nation breathed a collective sigh of relief at their safe release. Many people had attached yellow ribbons to trees and telephone poles to signal their support. Parades welcomed the hostages, neighbors and

Steven M. Gonzales, Andrew A. Ramirez, and Christopher J. Stone (left to right) are seen at a press conference just before being released by their Yugoslav captors.

friends rushed to their aid, and military physicians and psychiatrists stood ready to assist any who required help with the difficult transition back to normalcy.

Following his liberation along with the other fifty-one hostages, Bill Belk recalled the incredible boost to morale created by the nation's reaction during that ordeal. "It was probably about twenty-five miles or so to the hospital, and all along that route the streets were lined with cheering people." At the end of his journey an amazed Belk stared at "the huge number of letters that were waiting for us at the hospital. They had these letters stacked in boxes there in the hallway, and there were literally thousands and thousands of them."[2]

Unfortunately for the men of a prior era who battled Germany and Japan, these feelings were not as evident sixty years ago during World War II (1941–1945). Though mothers and fathers worried about the fate of their sons in that conflict with the same intensity as parents in later times, the nation's reaction differed. Media coverage in the 1940s could not bring the plight of prisoners to the nation with the same immediacy as it could in the 1970s or 1990s, when satellite-fed images reached the world's television screens minutes or hours after capture.

Instead of being aroused to anger by haunting faces plastered on television screens, Americans in the 1940s knew little of what their fathers, sons, brothers, uncles, and friends endured in German and Japanese prison camps. They could only hang on and hope that war's end would return their loved ones safe and whole.

Another reason for the different reaction was that the country had embarked upon a worldwide struggle to vanquish evil, personified by Germany and Japan. Toward that effort every American family contributed its labor, time, money, and in many circumstances, its sons. Since misfortune had become all too common, what happened to one family was not as shocking to others, since they had to deal with their own tribulations. The nation fretted over three captive soldiers in 1999 because they were the only Americans to suffer such a fate, but thousands of others endured similar misery in the 1940s. More than twenty-five thousand Americans wasted away in Japanese prison camps, while another ninety-five thousand languished inside German camps.

While the rest of the world focused upon titanic military clashes, those Americans who fell into German or Japanese hands drifted to the backwaters of the war. There, out of sight of their countrymen and with little contact with home, they began a second, more personal war. Rather than contested on a battlefield, this struggle occurred in sparse wooden barracks standing inside barbed wire enclosures. Rather than having news of his efforts triumphantly heralded by newspaper headlines and front-page stories, the prisoner waged his war in the shadows of obscurity, known only to himself and to others in the same circumstances.

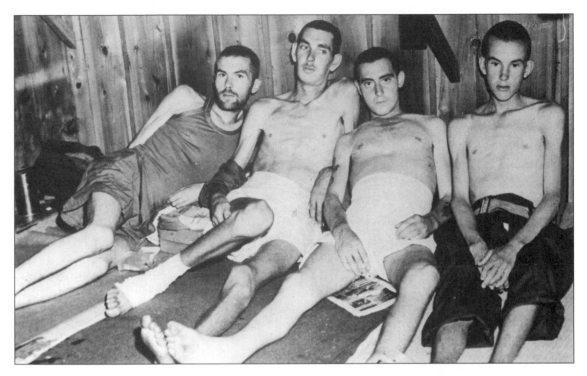

Four U.S. soldiers await medical attention after being liberated from a Japanese prison camp.

When the prisoners of war returned to a triumphant United States in 1945, they participated in parades, listened to speeches, and received honors just as every soldier did. A grateful nation welcomed home its soldiers with open arms, but when the military music, patriotic songs, and heartwarming words ended, the nation quickly diverted its attention from military to civilian matters. People wanted to raise families and resume careers. Interest in the war faded, and those who fought in it were left to their memories.

While many servicemen easily adjusted to peacetime in the United States, ex-prisoners of war encountered harsher times. In some ways they waged their third war. After fighting the enemy and then struggling

to remain alive during the rigors of prison camp existence, they now battled mental specters and coped with physical disabilities brought on by their incarceration. The military had not yet recognized the necessity for continued support. Frequently left to their own devices, some ex-prisoners of war floundered.

Caught by the enemy during war and cornered in a nightmarish world inside the prison camp, some now felt trapped at home. Unable to share memories with loved ones who could never completely understand, these men remained silent and suffered alone. Through the years more of the men have begun talking, but others still live in hushed silence, preferring to handle the demons in their own way.

Louis G. Grivetti, a prisoner of the Germans during the war's final six months, explained how he dealt with the situation. "When I came back to the States I just tried to forget everything about being a POW."[3]

From the moment of their capture, American prisoners of war stepped into an experience for which no amount of training could have prepared them. Brutal interrogations, forced winter marches, poor food, loneliness, humiliation, beatings, and death hounded them daily, and most reacted in noble ways. While glorious battlefield achievements justifiably continue

American troops captured by German forces are marched off to prison camp. Nothing could prepare them for the hardships they would face.

to gather attention, the war these men fought deserves equal notice.

10

Chapter 1

"You Sure Don't Want to Die"

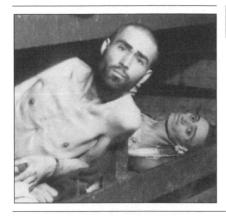

Captain Julius M. Green did not like his predicament. He and his unit had been pinned against the sea by advancing German forces, leaving them no escape route. They could only continue the fight and hope that relief arrived before the enemy.

The soldier cautiously stepped from position to position, checking on wounded comrades. As he turned a corner, he froze in his tracks. "I saw a tank, its gun pointing in my direction. The hatch opened and a character in dungarees emerged holding an automatic [pistol], which he pointed at me."

From his tank the German ordered his startled foe to surrender. Hopelessly trapped, the young soldier raised his hands. As the German walked toward him, he uttered words which thousands of American soldiers and airmen would hear over the course of two years. "For you the war is over,"[4] said the German.

Though the German correctly stated that the fighting war had ended for the young American, as a prisoner of war he would begin a new battle. During his incarceration he would struggle to retain dignity, maintain a semblance of health, and emerge unscarred. For him, this second war was far from over.

The Geneva Convention

In many ways a prisoner's fate depended upon where he was captured. In Europe, while there were instances of murder and severe abuse, generally the conditions were harsh but tolerable. In the Pacific, while there were instances of decency and kindness, generally the conditions were horrendous.

Rules and procedures for the treatment of prisoners of war existed, but they were not universally followed. On July 27, 1929, representatives from more than forty nations gathered in Geneva, Switzerland, to sign the Geneva Convention. This document of ninety-seven articles defined a prisoner of war as a member of a regular

Representatives from more than forty nations meet in Geneva to sign the Geneva Convention. The Convention dictated how prisoners of war should be treated.

military unit, wearing a uniform (thus spies were excluded). The Convention declared that a prisoner must be humanely treated and listed the rights of a prisoner and the duties of the captor.

For instance, the prisoners' food, clothing and shelter were to be comparable to what was provided to the captor's troops. Captors had to release lists of who they had taken prisoner and permit prisoners to communicate with their families. Officers (lieutenants, captains, majors, colonels, generals) could not be forced to do work, while enlisted ranks (privates, corporals, sergeants) could perform work as long as it did not endanger their health

or have anything to do with war operations.

Imprinting rules on a piece of paper does not guarantee that they will be followed, however. Though the International Red Cross was given the responsibility of inspecting prison camps as the war progressed, and though the Swiss government represented American interests in dealings with the Germans and Japanese, they had little actual power to enforce the Geneva Convention. Germany adhered more closely than Japan, but violations occurred in both areas. When American Private Harold J. Farrell and other prisoners complained to a German guard that their lengthy work schedule violated the Geneva Convention, the guard tapped his rifle and replied, "Here is my Geneva Convention."[5]

Capture in Japan

Because of the swiftness and the complete surprise with which the Japanese executed their initial attacks against the United States, most Americans who fell into Japanese hands were taken in the war's opening weeks in late 1941 and early 1942. After that, because of the Japanese code of military behavior and an American retaliation against it, few prisoners on either side were taken. Both the American and Japanese armies engaged in violent combat to the death in which they took no prisoners and did not expect to be taken as one.

Stories from escaped prisoners and earlier newspaper accounts of Japanese atrocities in China and Manchuria in the 1930s, where prisoners were routinely shot, stabbed, or beheaded, underscored the difference between the European and Pacific theaters. Lieutenant John W. Mahoney, pilot of a P-38 fighter, recalled his reaction when he learned he had been assigned to fight in Europe. "I was the most relieved guy around. No way did I want to fight in the Pacific if possible. The fighting was so brutal and they didn't take prisoners anyway. At least in Europe I figured I had a chance at

A Touching Farewell

Army radio operator Corporal Irving Strobing sent one of the war's most moving messages as the Japanese closed in on his position on Corregidor in the Philippines. With mere hours remaining before capture, Strobing dispatched over the airwaves his final thoughts, in hopes that someone in the United States would pick up the words. John Toland included the message in his book *But Not in Shame:*

> I know now how a mouse feels, caught in a trap and waiting for guys to come along and finish it up. My name is Irving Strobing. Get this to my mother, Mrs. Minnie Strobing, 605 Barbey Street, Brooklyn, New York. . . . My love to Pa, Joe, Sue, Mac, Carry, Joyce and Paul. Also to all family and friends. God bless 'em all. Hope they will be there when I come home. Tell Joe wherever he is to give 'em hell for us. God bless you.

U.S. troops surrender to the Japanese on Corregidor.

survival."[6] Mahoney had reason to appreciate his assignment—he was shot down and captured by German forces in December 1944.

Code of Bushido

Americans taken captive in the Pacific received harsh treatment because of how Japanese soldiers had been trained. Japanese soldiers were expect to act according to the high standards established in the code of conduct called Bushido, which means the "way of the warrior." Centered upon unquestioning loyalty, complete obedience, honor, and bravery, the code harkened to the days of the ancient samurai, Japan's revered soldier, who battled without fear of death. A Japanese soldier was expected to fight honorably, subsist on insufficient food and water without complaint, and above all never to surrender.

"Duty is weightier than a mountain, while death is lighter than a feather,"[7] admonished one portion of the code. The worst offense a Japanese soldier could commit was to surrender in battle. By this action he shamed his family and village, and his name would be removed from the town's registry.

A U.S. marine takes position next to a Japanese officer killed in battle. The code of Bushido required that a Japanese soldier fight to the death rather than surrender.

Since they heaped dishonor upon any of their own ranks who surrendered, Japanese soldiers viewed American prisoners of war as weak individuals who deserved nothing but contempt. The Japanese thought those who surrendered lost their rights as soldiers and so should expect inhumane treatment. While 4 percent of the Americans taken prisoner by the Germans died in captivity, more than 28 percent of the Americans captured by the Japanese died.

Pacific Shock and Shame

On the quiet morning of December 8, 1941, the U.S. gunboat USS *Wake* peacefully floated at its moor in the Whangpoo River in Shanghai, China. Deteriorating developments in the Far East indicated that war could erupt at any moment with the Japanese, so most American ships had departed Chinese waters, which the Japanese controlled, and headed for the Philippines. The *Wake* and one other American gunboat remained in China for the time being.

They would never reach the Philippines. Halfway across the Pacific Ocean in Hawaii, beyond the international date line, where it was still December 7, Japanese aircraft attacked the U.S. fleet in Pearl Harbor to start World War II. For the first time in a generation the United States was at war.

The men aboard the *Wake* did not yet realize this. Early that morning, as Americans battled in Hawaii, a Japanese craft silently inched near the *Wake*. Japanese poured onto the gunboat, surprised the crew, and demanded their surrender. Out-

Never Surrender

The Japanese soldier understood even before he entered the military that to surrender to the enemy was a humiliation for him and his entire family. In their informative history of the Japanese during World War II, *Japan at War: An Oral History*, Haruko Taya Cook and Theodore F. Cook include the comments of Yamauchi Takeo, a soldier who fought on Saipan.

In those days, Japanese soldiers really accepted the idea that they must eventually die. If you were taken alive as a prisoner you could never face your own family. They'd been sent off by their own neighbors [to enter the military] with cheers of *"Banzai!"* How could they now go home? "General attack" meant suicide. Those unable to move were told to die by a hand grenade or by taking cyanide [poison].

numbered and outgunned, the crew had no choice but to lay down their weapons. Only hours into World War II, the first American military personnel fell into enemy hands.

Farther to the north, 204 American marines stationed near Beijing and Tianjin, China, also surrendered to a stronger Japanese unit. The ordeal embarrassed the marines, who took pride in considering themselves an elite unit who could outfight anyone. Captain John A. White, the marine executive officer at Tianjin, trained his entire career to fight for his country, but before he could even remove his pistol from his holster, he had to surrender. As he later said, that first day of World War II contained "no shooting, no heroics nor great drama, only sorrow and frustration."[8]

The first Americans taken prisoner in World War II experienced different emotions than those captured later, especially by the Germans. With stunning rapidity, the Japanese swept to a convincing string of victories over American and British forces in the Pacific and Far East. These men struggled not simply with the specter of being captured but also with the unpleasant thought that they had been so convincingly overwhelmed by Japan, a nation previously regarded as inferior by the Americans and British. On top of humiliation, many were distraught that they could not mount a stronger defense.

Part of the reason lay in the fact that the men stationed in the Pacific and Far East had not been given adequate weaponry. The United States' military forces had diminished in size during the previous two decades as the nation turned its attention to domestic concerns, partially the Great Depression, which had cast millions of workers out of jobs. Money that normally would have gone to the military was instead shifted to civilian programs. As a result, American military forces had to make do with insufficient equipment until American factories could produce more.

One officer captured early in the war, Marine Commander Donald T. Giles Sr., wrote that the marines stationed at Guam, an island thirty-six hundred miles west of Hawaii, possessed only fifteen Browning automatic rifles, thirteen machine guns, some Colt .45 automatic pistols, and rifles so old that many had been "marked prominently FOR TRAINING ONLY—DO NOT FIRE." A frustrated Giles added, "Where were our defenses? There were none. No aircraft, no airfields—nothing but ancient small arms. All I had was my Colt .45. We were most poorly equipped to combat the seasoned, trained crack troops of our enemy. And after the surprise attack on Pearl Harbor, we were without hope of any relief from our fleet." [9]

In many instances the men who surrendered in the Pacific also had to face the emotionally devastating experience of watching their own flag—the Stars and Stripes—being pulled down and replaced by the Rising Sun flag of the Japanese. Giles never forgot that moment. "It was a sad sight to see the good old Stars and Stripes struck from the plaza flagpole and see the Rising Sun raised in its place." He explained that many of his fellow marines struggled to contain their emotions at seeing the American flag disappear, "a flag under which our forefathers had bled and died to keep our country free." [10]

In 1941 and early 1942, captured marine and army personnel suffered mental and physical scars which, in some cases, lasted for years after the war. Giles stated that many soldiers "felt and would feel for years thereafter that they had failed: that they had failed their country, their flag, and the traditions of the naval [and army] service; that they had failed the natives [of Guam] who had been entrusted to their care; that they had failed in their careers." [11]

The American flag is lowered on Corregidor. The sight of the Stars and Stripes being hauled down was a devastating one to the men who surrendered.

Capture in Europe

Prisoners of war were generally treated with some decency in Europe. Custom in both the German and American armies was to accept enemy soldiers' surrender and send them to the back lines for shipment to prison camp.

Exceptions to this practice existed. German soldiers shot on sight any American caught in possession of German-made items. They reasoned that if an American carried a German pistol, blanket, flag, or other product, he must have either killed a German soldier and removed the item from his body or scavenged souvenirs from dead German soldiers. After killing such Americans, Germans would sometimes slash huge Xs across their chests as a ghoulish warning to other Americans.

Most of the American prisoners of war seized in Europe were captured during four major campaigns. The American airmen who flew fighters and manned the huge bombers that pounded German forces were captured throughout the period from 1942 to 1945. Ground forces such as the infantry and tank crews tended to be captured in large numbers because of the huge military assaults in which they participated. The first group—almost two thousand men—was seized during the 1942 fighting in North Africa. Another twenty thousand fell into German hands during the invasion of Italy in 1943, while more than seventy-six thousand Americans were captured in France during the mammoth

D day (June 6, 1944) invasion and the subsequent fighting. Germany's last-ditch attempt to halt the American advance, the Battle of the Bulge in December 1944 produced twenty-three thousand prisoners in five weeks of fighting.

If an American prisoner was not cold-bloodedly gunned down by his captors in the first moments—which occurred on occasion in Europe and with frightening normality in the Pacific—he expected to survive until liberation.

"Good-bye to This World"

Both sides in the Pacific theater engaged in brutalities toward their opponents. In his book *Surrender and Survival: The Experience of American POWs in the Pacific, 1941–1945,* E. Bartlett Kerr quotes from a diary taken from a dead Japanese soldier who witnessed the execution of a downed American aviator in early 1943 in New Guinea.

He is apparently resigned. The precaution is taken of surrounding him with guards with fixed bayonets, but he remains calm. He even stretches out his neck and is very brave. When I put myself in the prisoner's place and think that in one more minute it will be good-bye to this world, although the daily [American] bombings have filled me with hate, ordinary human feelings make me pity him. The Tai [unit] commander has drawn his favorite sword. It is the famous Osamune sword which he showed us at the observation post. It glitters in the light and sends a cold shiver down my spine. He taps the prisoner's neck lightly with the back of the blade and then raises it above his head with both arms and brings it down with a sweep.

Depending upon the nature of the combat in which they participated, soldiers in Europe could be captured in any number of ways. On July 28, 1944, Corporal Harold W. Gattung walked on a night patrol with six other soldiers in Italy when "suddenly all hell broke loose. We were in the middle of a German ambush. The point man [the soldier walking ahead of the rest], our sergeant, and the last man in the column were killed immediately. I was the second man in the column and I dove off a ditch at the side of the road."[12] Gattung and three survivors, hopelessly surrounded, had little choice but to surrender.

During the D day invasion of June 1944, Private First Class Adam L. Canupp parachuted into France with the rest of his unit. Before they hit ground they encountered thick German fire which killed most of the men. According to Canupp, he and another man "made our way into a wooded area and stayed there until the next morning. Then we stayed hidden as much as possible because there were Germans all around us. A Frenchman spotted us and turned us in to the Germans. We were in a ditch, and I had fallen asleep. Something woke me up, and I looked up. My buddy was standing there with his hands up. We were captured by German paratroopers."[13]

Other men turned the corner of a French or Italian village street to find themselves staring at German rifles, cut off from the rest of their units by advancing German forces or lost behind German lines. Capture could occur anywhere at almost any time.

On its way to the front, a German tank passes a column of POWs during the Battle of the Bulge. Twenty-three thousand Americans were captured during the battle.

As in the Pacific, few had any alternative to surrender. Private First Class Johnnie C. Womble explained that when a unit of German Panzer tanks trapped his unit, "I always said that I would never surrender, but you sure don't want to die. We finally either had to die or surrender, and our commander decided that we should give up."[14]

Two groups of Americans feared capture more than any others—those of Jewish background and airmen, particularly those who flew the massive bombers which wreaked so much destruction on German towns and civilians. German leader Adolf Hitler's brutal treatment of Jews was well documented, and every Jewish American

worried about his fate should he fall into German hands.

Bomber pilot Matthew Radnossky took the precaution of having different dog tags made. The nameplates dangling from chains around soldiers' necks not only identified them by name but also contained a letter indicating religious affiliation. Whenever his mission took him over Germany, Radnossky replaced the small metallic plate which bore the letter "J," indicating he was

Jewish inmates look out from their barracks in a concentration camp. Jewish Americans had reason to fear being captured by the Germans.

Jewish, with one bearing the letter "P," meaning Protestant. When he was subsequently shot down, his captors did not realize he was Jewish.

Later in the war American airmen had more reason to worry, because if they parachuted from a damaged aircraft, they might land somewhere in the vicinity of the area they had just bombed. German civilians, increasingly enraged that their homes and businesses had been destroyed and friends and loved ones had been maimed or killed, sometimes charged the airmen, wrenched them away from German soldiers, and hanged them or hacked them to pieces.

For those who survived the first few moments of captivity, Americans in the Pacific and European theaters now started the next phase of their harsh journey—interrogation and transport to prison camp.

Chapter 2

"Guests for an Indefinite Stay"

When an American fell into enemy hands, he often received a speedy indication that his life would never be the same. In Europe, at least, he retained hope of decent treatment. Such was not the case in the Pacific.

A Harsh Reception

German soldiers seized Corporal Robert Engstrom on December 17, 1944, during intense fighting along the Belgian-French border in the Battle of the Bulge. They led him to a farmhouse, where a German officer grabbed him by the shirt, cracked him between the eyes, and threw him down a flight of stairs. Before he could recover, a second German severely beat him. Like countless other prisoners of war, Engstrom faced the unpleasant thought that by surrendering, his fate rested with men whom he had been trying to kill only moments before.

Engstrom survived the war; many others did not. Another American soldier fighting in the Battle of the Bulge, James Graff, re-

called learning that six Americans "who were captured had been found shot to death by a small arms bullet in the head or heart."[15]

The most hideous incident involving American prisoners of war in Europe occurred on the same day that Engstrom surrendered. Hopelessly trapped by a superior German force of infantry and tanks, 130 Americans surrendered near Malmédy, Belgium, not far from the German border. The men were taken to nearby fields, lined up in eight rows, and machine-gunned. For fifteen minutes bullets riddled the helpless Americans, and passing German units fired into the heaps of bodies. Miraculously, some Americans survived and hid underneath the bodies of their slain comrades, but even that did not assure their safety.

First Lieutenant Virgil Lary lay breathlessly still among the dead as a German soldier walked up and shot the man lying next to him in the head. "I lay tensely still, expecting the end. Could he

see me breathing? Could I take a kick in the groin without wincing?"[16]

The German moved on. Lary remained motionless until nightfall, when he and a handful of Americans fled into the woods. They eventually rejoined their units and spread news of the infamous incident. In retaliation, for the remainder of the Battle of the Bulge, many American units refused to take German prisoners. Instead, they shot surrendering Germans.

Most Americans survived capture in Europe. Prisoners of war were usually ques-

The bodies of U.S. prisoners slaughtered by German troops lie in the snow near Malmédy.

tioned soon after their seizure. German interrogators hoped to gather information on the men's units, their objectives, and their commanding officers, and they searched the Americans for letters, maps, and diaries that might provide more material. According to the Geneva Convention, the prisoner was only required to give his name, rank, and serial number, but interrogators employed many tricks, some more brutal than others, to get the Americans talking.

The German Luftwaffe (air force) ran an interrogation center at Oberursel, northwest of Frankfurt. By 1944 more than three hundred interrogators questioned two thousand Americans each month. The Germans relied mainly upon mind games—engaging in a friendly chat about baseball or Hollywood movie stars to get the men to re-

lax, then springing military questions on them—rather than physical intimidation, although violence was never completely out of the picture. The Germans wanted to learn which American captives might be willing to cooperate by writing propaganda

John W. Mahoney was taken prisoner when his P-38 was shot down over Europe. His German captors prepared this identification sheet.

leaflets, listening in on prison conversations and reporting what they heard to German authorities, or broadcasting radio appeals to surrender.

If they knew that an American was Jewish, they made sure to build upon his fears of what the Nazis might do to him. When Sergeant Daniel Abeles, a gunner on a B-17 bomber and a Jew, sat down for questioning, the German facing him menacingly inquired, "You know what is done with Jews here?"[17] The interrogator led Abeles to believe that he would soon be shot, but after a few questions the German sent him back to his quarters.

Many Americans at Oberursel encountered the skilled interrogator Hans Scharff. He spoke perfect English and read every American newspaper he could acquire, so he knew American mannerisms and what might be effective. Scharff normally put the American on the defensive by stating early in the questioning that he suspected the American was a spy and thus would be handed over to the Gestapo. Scharff figured that would open the mouths of some Americans.

If that did not work, Scharff involved the prisoner in idle chatter to lower his defenses and then tried to draw out information from the relaxed individual. He frequently offered small rewards to Americans who cooperated, such as a hot meal, and made it widely known that those who proved difficult would be sent to solitary confinement, which was a dark, damp cell in which a prisoner was confined for days. Ger-

man guards regulated the tiny cell's temperature so that it alternately fell below freezing for long stretches, then soared to almost unbearable heat.

A captured American pilot, Captain John A. Vietor, wrote an account of his interrogation by a German major. The German officer offered Vietor a cigarette, then communicated in excellent English.

"Captain, where are your identification tags, your dog tags?"

"I forgot to wear them."

"How do I know you are not a saboteur without your identification?" When the German pressed Vietor to divulge his squadron, Vietor gave only his name, rank, and serial number.

Acting displeased, the German warned that if Vietor could give no additional information, "I may be compelled to turn you over to the Gestapo for investigation."[18] His threats did not intimidate the silent Vietor, who was returned unharmed to his cell.

Americans were surprised at how much information the Germans already possessed. When Corporal Robert Engstrom failed to cooperate, a German officer "then told me he knew everything about us. He told me I had been captured on December 17, and that I was in the 32nd Cavalry. He even knew how many casualties we had suffered and how many of us had been captured."[19]

Two days after Vietor's interrogation the major handed him a slip of paper with the identification of his unit. Vietor listened as the major recited the name of Vietor's commander, where he had attended college, and his military posts throughout the 1930s. Another American, airman Alexander Jefferson, sat stunned while his German interrogator opened an enormous book containing Jefferson's school records, his father's social security number, and even photos of Jefferson.

Good Guy/Bad Guy

Most soldiers and airmen in Europe were warned that if captured by the Germans, they might be subject to the "good guy/bad guy" interrogation technique. In this maneuver, one man would threaten the prisoner with execution or torture, then a more friendly German would enter, try to make the American relax, and attempt to gain valuable information from him. Second Lieutenant Phil Miller recounts his experience in Lewis H. Carlson's *We Were Each Other's Prisoners*, a book of interviews with prisoners of war.

> My first interrogator had me pretty well convinced that in spite of my forewarning he was going to execute me. He went into a towering rage. He called me a spy and saboteur and told me execution was what I deserved. I decided that when I got in front of the firing squad, I would begin talking my head off but not before they pointed their rifles at me. The second man was as friendly as predicted. He told me all about himself, how he had worked in the U.S. as a traveling salesman in Tennessee and so forth. He said it was true that I was suspected of being a saboteur with a false serial number and rank, and that they needed additional information to verify my true identification.

Miller refused to answer any questions, and after three or four more interrogations, he was sent to prison camp.

Surrendering Did Not Seem Reasonable

Conditions were dramatically more hideous in the Pacific. John Podelesny, a marine on Guam, stood in line with forty other American prisoners as the Japanese searched them for valuables. The Japanese employed sign language and pointed with their bayonets to indicate they wanted the Americans to remove their shirts, trousers, and shoes, but the marine standing next to Podelesny was slow in reacting. A Japanese soldier quickly stepped up to the man and ran his bayonet through his stomach. Staring at the dead marine, Podelesny began realizing the seriousness of his predicament.

Not far from Podelesny, Commander Donald Giles observed another Japanese captor bayoneting an American named Kauffman, "ripping the sharp blade from one side of his belly to the other. Two of his buddies instinctively stepped forward and were decapitated [their heads cut off] instantly. Shortly thereafter, two Japanese soldiers dragged Kauffman's gutted body from where he had fallen and threw it onto a nearby trash heap."[20]

Seeing such atrocities alerted Giles, Podelesny, and others captured in the Pacific that they could expect no mercy. "Surrendering did not seem to be a reasonable alternative,"[21] Giles later explained.

Since fewer American infantrymen fell into Japanese hands as the war progressed, Japanese interrogators focused on downed American airmen and crew members from submarines. American prisoners dreaded

A Japanese soldier displays the severed head of a Chinese prisoner he has executed. Americans could also expect no mercy if they were captured by the Japanese.

Navy aviator Lieutenant Stefen A. Nyarady arrived at Ofuna in late 1943 after being shot down north of New Guinea. The Japanese asked him about his ship, but when he failed to respond they repeatedly whacked him with a baseball bat. They continued this treatment over the next nine months before he was transferred to another location.

The Japanese were especially eager to learn the maximum diving depth of American submarines, which had inflicted enormous damage on Japanese shipping and severely cut the flow of goods into and out of the Japanese home islands. Japanese ships needed that knowledge so they could accurately set the depth charges with which they attacked American submarines.

Transported to Camp

Following interrogation, American prisoners of war were taken to a prison camp. For most, their first stop was a temporary camp not far from where they had been seized. From there they headed by train, ship, truck, or foot to the first of two or more different prison camps. The Geneva Convention required that warring nations clearly mark on the vehicles or ships that they contained prisoners of war so that aircraft or submarines would not attack, but this was usually ignored by Germany and Japan.

the center at Ofuna, Japan, known to Americans as the Torture Farm because of the brutal methods used to gain information. The Japanese routinely beat the prisoners, bayoneted many, or shoved bamboo splinters under their fingernails.

Germany maintained more than one hundred camps to house American captives. Most German camps were called Stalag, meaning Main Camp, or Stalags Luft, which incarcerated captured airmen. Though a handful of camps existed in Poland and Austria, the vast majority were in Germany, with ninety, and Italy, with twenty-one.

Camps stood in the middle of dense forests, on the mountains, or on isolated promontories. While a few were in warm climates, 95 percent experienced brief summers followed by harsh winters, similar to weather in Canada.

The Germans placed Corporal Engstrom into a boxcar called a "forty-and-eight" (large enough for either forty men or eight horses). He was given one-third of a loaf of bread and half a tin of cheese for the seven-day trip to Stalag XIIIC near Hammelburg, Germany.

American POWs walk about the grounds of a Stalag in northern Germany. They are wearing heavy coats to keep out the winter cold.

Private Lawrence E. Roberts and other prisoners of war marched toward Germany for five days from where they had been captured in northern France in July 1944. The Germans marched them at night to avoid strafing by Allied aircraft and herded the prisoners in schoolhouses and vacant buildings by day.

Captain Vietor traveled by train to Munich, Germany, where the hostility from German civilians as he was marched through the train station surprised him. Women called the airmen murderers and spat at them. "This was the first time where we had encountered hatred and bitterness against Allied flyers. For our own protection we were shoved down a cellar beneath the station where we waited until midnight; then we were switched to another train."[22]

Japanese Camps

While most German prison camps were at about the same latitude, Japanese camps dotted all reaches of the Pacific Rim. Some lay in the tropics where soldiers battled a blazing sun and withering heat, while others

Heading to Camp

For many Americans captured in Europe, an unpleasant trip to camp by railroad awaited. The small boxcars, sometimes filthy from previous use, offered little room for the large groups of captives shoved inside. Captured on September 11, 1944, Private First Class Johnnie C. Womble recorded his experience aboard a train headed for Stalag XIIA near Limburg, Germany for a book edited by Harry Spiller, *Prisoners of Nazis: Accounts by American POWs in World War II.*

The cars were "forty and eights." There was horse manure and straw a good six inches deep on the floor of the cars from horses the Germans had transported by train. We were so crowded in the car that we couldn't clear a spot to sleep, so we just had to lay in the manure. Some of the guys tried to punch holes in the bottom of the car to get rid of some of it, but they weren't able to.

The trip took us four days and nights. There were no toilets, so if you had to relieve yourself you just had to go on the floor. . . . We were bombed and strafed every day by our own planes because they didn't know we were a POW train."

Many prisoners were transported to camp in boxcars such as this one.

were in the cold climates of Manchuria, China, and northern Japan. Thus an American seized at Wake Island and dressed for the tropics might have ended up in snow-covered terrain. The Japanese home islands contained 176 prison camps, while another five hundred were established on Pacific islands and the Asian mainland. Most Americans spent the war either in the Philippines, the Japanese home islands, or Manchuria.

Commander Giles and other marine and navy personnel taken on Guam in the Pacific remained on the island for a month before they were shipped to Japan. The circumstances inside the transport were far from pleasant, although they proved to be better than those experienced by most of his compatriots.

> In the hold we were kept cramped on six-tiered shelves, with eight men lying side by side on each shelf. There was little space between one's face and the shelf above, and there was no room to move. Perhaps worse was the total lack of ventilation and the virtual lack of sanitation in the hold.[23]

Giles ate from buckets that the Japanese guards lowered into the hold from above. The food was so bad that a fellow prisoner muttered he would not feed it to his hogs back home. When the ship arrived in Japan, Giles and the others cheered up when they received a cup of hot water, a piece of bread, and an orange. However, the fruit was snatched away from the prisoners as soon as

Japanese newsmen, on hand to record the "excellent" treatment of prisoners by the Japanese, left to record their stories.

The Bataan Death March

One of the most notorious events of World War II, or of any war for that matter, occurred in April 1942. American military forces in the Philippines had surrendered to the Japanese army, who now had the responsibility of moving these captive soldiers out of the combat zone and into camps. Hastily drawn plans called for trains to transport the prisoners to Camp O'Donnell in the Philippines after they had marched from their point of capture to Balanga, a location requiring almost a twenty-mile hike for some men. Poor planning led to confusion and inadequate food and rest stops. Brutality by some Japanese guards led to shock, horror, and death.

"My first realization this was going to be a tough ordeal was that initial day," recalled Staff Sergeant William Nolan. "Some American officers tried to organize us and get us some food, but they were either beaten or killed so we shut up. The word passed down the line to get rid of Japanese money or souvenirs, because that meant instant death if they found it on you."[24]

Groups of as many as three hundred prisoners started filtering out of Mariveles on Bataan's southern edge on April 10. As they inched north, Japanese troops moving in the opposite direction stopped to loot or beat the prisoners. Nolan learned to be especially wary of passing Japanese trucks,

After the fall of the Philippines, U.S. soldiers are herded toward captivity. Hundreds would not survive what soon became known as the Bataan Death March.

since their occupants often tried to smack American prisoners with their rifles. He marched hour after hour on a dusty road without water to quench a torturous thirst aggravated by the ninety-five degree heat. More than once, fellow sufferers dashed from the line toward nearby water, only to be shot dead within a few paces.

Though stops dotted the march, they hardly eased the prisoners' discomfort. A rice paddy enclosed by barbed wire housed the prisoners at Orani, eleven miles from Balanga. As each group passed through, the field became so foul with human waste that an overwhelming stench greeted prisoners before they reached the town's borders. At Lubao, a city of thirty thousand inhabitants sixteen miles farther along the trail, prisoners stumbled into a large tin building, oppressively hot from the burning sun, that contained one water spigot for all the men. San Fernando, an important rail center nine miles from Lubao, offered the final resting place. Reached by an asphalt road warmed by the sun and churned into jagged chunks by passing trucks and tanks, groups of prisoners passed through San Fernando for two weeks on their way to the boxcars which would take them to prison camp.

Above all, no matter how hot, how tired, how scared they became, the men knew they had to keep moving, for to fall behind was to die by bayonet or gunshot. One soldier gazed in horror as a guard tossed a sick American into the path of an onrushing string of tanks. After ten tanks had sped over the spot, "there was no way you could tell there'd ever been a man there. . . . The man disappeared, but his uniform had been pressed until it had become part of the ground."[25]

Thus the struggle boiled down to sick, weakened men, laboring in withering heat simply to stay on their feet. Already blistering when the prisoners started each morning, the unforgiving sun intensified through the day and transformed the roads into suffocating, dust-covered paths of agony.

"The roads were so dusty we looked like we had pancake on," related Nolan.

Malaria and dysentery further messed the road. We plowed along, like cattle, and played mental tricks with our-

Friendly Guards

Not every Japanese guard on the Death March beat or killed American soldiers. As E. Bartlett Kerr recounted in his book, *Surrender and Survival: The Experience of American POWs in the Pacific, 1941-1945*, some Americans encountered charitable soldiers. One guard slowed the pace and frequently halted his group to give the Americans much-needed rest. When as thanks some Americans tried to hand him a wristwatch and money, the guard refused. He told the men that he was a soldier and "a gentleman like yourselves."

Staff Sergeant Harold Feiner suffered from leg wounds, so the march almost was more than he could bear. One night, however, as he rested for a few moments, a Japanese guard quietly handed Feiner a cup of chocolate. "I hadn't had any food and no water for days. I didn't speak one single word of Japanese then, but he could speak a little English, but with a really horrible accent. 'Someday me go to Hollywood, me going to be a movie star.'"

During the remainder of that night the guard brought Feiner whatever food he could locate. Partially as a result of the Japanese guard's kindness, Feiner survived the Death March and the war.

American prisoners are allowed to rest during the Death March.

selves by thinking that something better waited for us just up the road. Every once in awhile, if the guards weren't looking and there was some water by the road, we'd try to quickly scoop some up, even though we could see dead Americans lying in it.[26]

As the weary, ragged line of prisoners meandered up the Bataan Peninsula, American and Filipino bodies lying in ditches alongside the road—many beheaded—became a more frequent sight. One American officer counted twenty-seven headless bodies before forcing himself to think about something else. From then on he walked with his eyes staring straight ahead. Inured to atrocities by marching hour after hour in the numbing sun, men learned to ignore such ghastly spectacles.

Many men attributed survival, in part, to comradeship with a few close buddies. Even for those who could not continue, or who were in the final hours of life, the presence of a friend alleviated the pain. One corporal observed some of his fellow soldiers in their last moments and noticed, "To have at least one close friend, a buddy to hold you in his arms and comfort you as you died, was enough."[27]

"We tried to help each other," mentioned Sergeant Joseph Kutch, commander of a Corregidor gun crew,

A man on each side of someone in danger of collapsing would prop him up. Four of us stuck together and shared anything we had with each other. In fact, the four of us ended up staying together throughout the entire war. I think we survived because we were so tight and helped each other.[28]

Some lost the strength and will to continue. As Private First Class John Falconer said, "Death was easier than life. All I had to do was just lay back and die. I didn't have to worry about that. It was as easy as letting go of a rope. A lot of people quit hanging on."[29]

Often the survivors of the Death March and prison camps claim that hatred kept them alive. Passion roused the spirit and gave purpose to life, while those who lacked emotion often succumbed.

"I stayed alive because I kept telling myself I would make it, that I could take anything the Japanese could give me,"[30] stated William Nolan.

Kutch put it more bluntly: "It was hatred of the Japanese that made me survive. I hated the Japanese so much, and I was determined to get them back."[31]

Arriving in Camp

Captain John Vietor's experience typified what happened to Americans when they first arrived at a German prison camp. The Germans shipped him to Stalag Luft I near Barth in northern Germany. Vietor and the others in his group were marched to a square brick building and ordered to remove their clothes. After guards tossed the clothes into one of three enormous caul-

Near the end of the Death March, prisoners use slings to carry those too weak to walk.

drons to delouse (remove lice from) the apparel, they divided the men into groups of twenty and lined them up for showers. Each man received a cake of soap and two minutes for what Vietor described as "delectable hot water, followed by one minute of cold." The brief shower "was ecstasy after weeks of grime, filth and stubble." Guards returned the men to the first room, where they donned their freshly deloused clothes, then shunted Vietor and the others to their barracks, which they would call home until liberated late in the war. "We were now guests of the Germans for an indefinite stay at their 'Country Club on the Baltic,' the well-known resort spa, Stalag Luft I, Barth, Germany." [32]

Prisoners of war in Japan would have willingly traded places with their compatriots languishing in Germany. In almost every instance, when a new group of American prisoners arrived at a camp, the Japanese commander lined them up, sometimes for hours in the blazing sun, then read a lengthy list of rules. Failure to abide by the regulations could result in immediate execution.

A Christmas to Forget

Private First Class Glenn C. Miller spent Christmas 1944 as a prisoner in a boxcar as it headed toward Germany. The unsanitary conditions and lack of food dampened spirits, but a few men attempted to spread a bit of Christmas cheer. In Lewis H. Carlson's book, *We Were Each Other's Prisoners*, Miller explained what happened.

I spent Christmas in that boxcar. There was no heat or water. The Germans would not let us out to relieve ourselves so everybody went to the bathroom in their steel helmets. . . . Some of the guys tried to sing Christmas carols. They would sing a few words, but then nothing. There was just no spirit to go on. It was a pretty miserable Christmas, but even at my lowest, I never got to the point where I no longer gave a damn. I thought I would make it.

At Zentsuji Prison Camp in Japan, Commander Giles and other men seized at Guam listened as the Japanese officer told them "you must do away with the false superiority complex that you seem to have been entertaining towards the Asiatic people."[33] Other rules stipulated that Americans must bow whenever they approached a Japanese soldier, that they must not try to escape, and that death would result for those showing antagonism or opposition.

The men had to strip, as was the case with Vietor in Germany, but rather than a hot shower the Americans watched Japanese guards ransack their clothing for any valuables that had not already been taken. Once this inspection ended, the Americans put on their clothes and were led to their barracks.

Most men in Germany and Japan, though they thought of eventual escape, realized the difficulty of such an enormous task. Giles spotted barbed wire atop each outside wall at Zentsuji and concluded that the notion of escape was not only ludicrous but also impractical. Even if he successfully broke out of camp, he would find himself trapped in a society whose language he neither spoke, read, nor understood. Besides, his very appearance would give him away in the Oriental nation.

With the grim knowledge that they had likely arrived at their home for an indefinite period of time, the American POWs began adjusting to their new surroundings.

Chapter 3

"Home Away from Home"

Many camps housed American prisoners of war in the European and Pacific theaters. Captain John Vietor's initial view of his prison camp, Stalag Luft I, was hardly reassuring. Resting on a marshy point of land in northern Germany near the Baltic Sea, Stalag Luft I was boxed in by the sea to the north and towering pine forests to the south. "Cold, damp fogs rolled in from the Baltic alternating with bleak, chilling winds," wrote Vietor. "Windswept, sandy and desolate, the peninsula was an isolated cul-de-sac [dead-end] of the war."[34]

One mile southeast stood the ancient town of Barth, a small fishing village with a thirteenth-century church. The prisoners in Stalag Luft I experienced brief summers and long, bitter winters that brought darkness by 3:00 P.M.

The camp typified many German prison camps. Two rings of barbed wire fencing, separated by up to fifty yards, enclosed the captives. Inside were the compounds, consisting of huge parade grounds circled by barracks in which the prisoners lived. A hospital stood between the two barbed wire rings.

Guard towers stood at regular intervals along the barbed wire fences. They were manned by German guards with orders to shoot any prisoner who approached the fence. To prevent escape by tunneling, the Germans planted listening devices in the ground and below barracks, and vicious attack dogs prowled the grounds.

Stalag Luft I contained four different compounds, each holding about twenty-five hundred prisoners. While Americans formed the largest block of prisoners, the camp also housed fifteen hundred British, French, Polish, and Canadian soldiers. Two thousand Russian captives lived in more inhumane conditions in one of the compounds. The Soviet Union had not signed the Geneva Convention, and because German soldiers knew that Russian soldiers brutally mistreated German captives, the Russian prisoners faced daily abuse.

Each of the four compounds contained twelve to fourteen wooden barracks called blocks. About fifty feet wide and two hundred feet long, the blocks held ten to twelve rooms, each of which had a stove, a table, a few chairs, and wooden double-decker beds. Burlap mattresses, alive with bedbugs, were supported by four wooden planks. To hold the few valuables they might have, inmates fashioned rough shelves from Red Cross parcels and placed them at the head of the beds. A few lockers for storing such items as knives, forks, and bowls might adorn the room, and lines of string above the beds held drying laundry. A solitary twenty-watt light bulb provided inadequate illumination.

Two additional buildings completed the compound. A kitchen provided food and hot water, while another building served as a combination chapel and theater. Each Sunday, services were held for Protestant, Catholic, and Jewish inmates by chaplains who had been seized.

German camps set up for officers were better organized and enjoyed superior conditions than those camps for enlisted men. At Stalag XIIIC the enlisted men slept on the floor of a stable. The latrine was simply an open hole in the ground, and the daily

In German prison camps, living conditions for officers (below) were better than those endured by enlisted men (left).

ration of food was soup and a piece of bread.

Japanese Prison Camps

In Japan, Commander Donald Giles faced worse conditions than Vietor. While life was more tolerable in the summer, Giles arrived in the middle of winter and wrote years later,

> I believe that if all of the prisoners who were at Zentsuji could be polled as to what they remember most about their introduction to Japan, they would agree that it was the cold. Coming from a tropical climate and having only tropical uniforms, we suffered horribly. We arrived in mid-January, and words cannot describe how desperately cold we were.[35]

Barbed wire surrounded the camp. One gate opened to the enclosure, which was closely guarded by many Japanese soldiers. After Giles walked through the main gate, soldiers led him and the others to one of the two-story wooden barracks in which he would live. While he occupied one room with seven other officers, enlisted men had to share the same space with thirteen others.

Each room measured about twenty feet square and had wooden sleeping platforms about eighteen inches above the floor. A paper-thin straw mat served as a mattress, and hard Japanese-style pillows filled with straw or rice husks made sleeping awkward. As their bodies became thinner from lack of

Topcoats and Blankets

Commander Donald T. Giles spent the war in Japanese prison camps. In his powerful memoir published long after the war, *Captive of the Rising Sun*, Giles explains what most men wore during their confinement in Japan.

> We wore our overcoats all the time, even in bed. On the day after our arrival we had been issued thin, working topcoats, which we wore nearly twenty-four hours a day, and khaki-colored ersatz blankets. I say ersatz because there was no sign of any wool in them. They consisted of cotton netting that had been impregnated with bits of paper. So at nighttime, still wearing our overcoats, we would roll ourselves up in these paper-filled blankets and try to retain all the body heat we could. If you could get close to the hibachi, you could get a little warm, either on one end or the other, depending upon how you were facing.

nourishment, the hard boards of the sleeping shelves scraped their skin whenever they turned.

A mess table and two benches stood in the room's center, leaving little space for each man. "Such crowded conditions were not conducive to harmonious relations with bunk- or camp-mates. Sleeping would have been easier with only six men to a shelf. With eight, each man had only about twenty-four inches of space."[36]

Tiny Japanese hibachis—ceramic pots holding a few bits of charcoal—provided minimal heat for the rooms. The men took turns huddling near the hibachis for warmth, but they had to breathe charcoal fumes which caused headaches.

Bathroom facilities were nothing more than open concrete pits and troughs called latrines, which were dug near the barracks. Thus the men endured biting cold during the winter and appalling stench and thousands of flies in the humid summer months.

In the Philippines and other tropical zones, prisoners did not have to face harsh winters, but the continuous sun made life almost as intolerable. They generally lived in bamboo barracks housing about sixty men, and wore burlap sacks when their uniforms wore thin.

Life for a Prisoner

In both German and Japanese camps, life gradually settled into a routine. Roll calls occurred every morning and evening, when camp guards lined up all the prisoners and laboriously counted each one to make sure no man was missing. If the guards miscounted or thought that someone had escaped, they recounted the men. Each prisoner had to stand in line during the entire process, which could take up to two hours or more in all sorts of extreme weather.

Men in both German and Japanese camps suffered similar indignities. Captain Vietor recalled standing through as many as ten recounts at Stalag Luft I. A prisoner of war in the Pacific explained later that "first, there was one man too many, then one man too few; thus the men be-

gan each day exhausted from the endless standing while the guard ran nervously up and down the lineup, constantly mumbling numbers. In the evening, it was the same thing again, the never-ending count . . . when what all the men wanted was supper and sleep." [37]

In Germany, a prisoner's fate after morning roll call depended upon who ran the camp. German camps supervised by veteran combat soldiers or by officers of the German air force, called the Luftwaffe, were usually administered more efficiently and adhered more strictly to the Geneva Convention. If other branches of the German military supervised the camp, such as diehard Nazi troops, treatment deteriorated.

Officers occupied their days in any number of ways. Since the Geneva Con-

American prisoners of war in Germany were often treated more harshly in camps supervised by hardened Nazi troops.

vention forbade manual labor for officers in prison camps, daily life was less physically arduous for them. They organized camp activities, regulated affairs among barracks, and enforced discipline among the troops to ensure some form of order.

Enlisted men faced a tougher time, for they could be put to work, as long as the labor had no connection to the war effort. This, like many articles of the Geneva Convention, was conveniently overlooked in many cases. Corporal Harold W. Gattung picked potatoes in German fields from daylight to sunset, while other enlisted men worked in German armaments factories or rebuilt roads.

Private Walter F. Gurley provides a typical example of the type of work performed by enlisted men. After capture by the Germans, he worked in a sawmill until bombs from an American air raid destroyed it. The Germans shifted him to another town, where he and other men scraped old mortar off bricks and rebuilt a theater that had been damaged. They labored on the theater for weeks, and on the first night after they completed construction, to Gurley's delight, British aircraft bombed and demolished it.

Prisoners under Japanese control had to work. In May 1942 the country's prime minister announced a policy of "No work— no food." He argued that since much of the nation existed under that rule, so should

Captured U.S. sailors and soldiers labor on Corregidor under the direction of Japanese guards.

prisoners of war. Enlisted men built bridges, repaired airfields, and worked in shipyards, factories, and mines. Officers worked too, but usually at chores requiring less exertion, such as raising chickens or tending a garden.

The most infamous construction project labored on by American and other prisoners involved the massive Burma-Siam railway. Cut through nearly impassable jungle which hid exotic animals and deadly diseases, American and British prisoners moved earth with picks and shovels so the Japanese could connect two vital areas by railway. Watched by whip-bearing Japanese guards, the prisoners hoisted baskets of dirt to their shoulders and hacked a path through the vines and branches to build the railroad bed. Working sixteen-hour days with inadequate nourishment and battling malaria and cholera, the prisoners completed the railway in November 1943. An average of four hundred prisoners died for each of the railway's 250 miles, including two hundred Americans.

Camp Organization

To create uniformity out of chaos, Americans in both German and Japanese camps created governing institutions that set rules, established order among the prisoners, and maintained as much military discipline as possible. The organizations purposely mirrored what the men experienced in the American military in order to make them feel both more accountable and more comfortable.

In Stalag Luft I, for example, the highest ranking officer appointed four wing commanders, each in charge of his own compound (or groups). The barracks within each compound were called squadrons, and the rooms in the barracks were termed flights.

American officers staffed four departments to administer American prisoners. A personnel division maintained accurate files on who was in camp, how they were captured, and how they conducted themselves while in camp. The intelligence unit gathered material on the war's progress and information that could help a prisoner escape. It also collected items that could be used in escape attempts, such as radio parts and German uniforms. The operations division created plans for major events, such as

A Deck of Cards!

Like all prisoners of war, Staff Sergeant William Nolan eagerly looked forward to packages from home. He received few Red Cross parcels throughout the war, and of the numerous packages mailed from Michigan by his mother, he obtained only one. In an interview with the author, Nolan mentioned the moment:

> I got this one package in March 1944. I anxiously ripped open the package, only to find a deck of cards. I remember thinking, "Damn it! Here I'm starving to death and they send me a deck of cards." I just tossed them aside.

> Well, a couple of weeks later a friend of mine asked to use the cards and when we opened up the deck, neatly tucked between the cards were five pictures of my parents and my five brothers and sisters.

what to do should their captors begin a mass execution or evacuation, and how to react to their liberation. A fourth division organized all food, clothing, and equipment that arrived in camp from the International Red Cross.

The Americans often engaged in secret activities, such as digging tunnels or discussing escape plans. Whenever they did, a man stood watch in each block for approaching Germans. When a guard turned the corner, the lookout shouted a quick warning, usually "Goon up!" to give his comrades time to stop what they were doing, hide any material, and act like they were playing cards or chatting. If an inquisitive German wondered what "Goon" meant, which was the derogatory word Americans used for the Germans, the Americans answered that it stood for "German Officer or Non-com."

Whenever new American prisoners arrived, the other Americans in camp put them through a rigorous procedure. First, the fresh arrivals were isolated in a room until their backgrounds could be verified, because the Germans sometimes planted spies among the prisoners. Then they were warned not to say anything to anyone. When Captain Vietor entered Stalag Luft I, an American officer admonished him and his group to say nothing about their units or role in the war because a German plant might be among them. The officer added, "The Germans aren't the only ones who can take disciplinary action. Keep your mouths shut!"[38]

If an inmate talked too freely, his superiors placed the information in his personnel file, and camp officers made sure the talkative individual received the least desirable work details.

"Never Did I Get Enough to Eat"

Though some camps provided more food than others, no prisoner of war emerged healthier than when he entered. The normal ration in German camps neared fifteen hundred calories per day (less than half the normal recommended diet), while the amount was less in Japanese camps. The meager calories meant that most prisoners lost at least thirty five pounds.

"Never during my captivity did I get enough to eat,"[39] claimed one soldier of his time in Germany. Vietor wrote that each day eight men received one loaf of moldy, black bread, made partially with sawdust to give it bulk. Potatoes and barley supplemented their diets.

"I liked the barley," claimed Vietor, "even the little white bugs that went with it. By mixing it with corned beef and covering it with sugar [from Red Cross parcels], a revolting combination to think about now, it was quite palatable. Besides, barley bugs were supposed to contain vitamins."[40]

In late 1942 Japanese officials established the amount of food for each prisoner. Officers received a daily allotment of fifteen ounces of rice or barley, while enlisted men received twenty to twenty-seven

These American POWs were freed from a Japanese-run camp in the Philippines. Each had lost fifty to sixty pounds during captivity.

ounces because their work was harder. If available, a few vegetables and even bits of meat would be handed out, but at best the allowance was half what an American soldier received during peacetime duty. Japan claimed that prisoners were given the same amounts as Japanese soldiers, which could be true in some locations, but the average Japanese soldier was smaller than his American counterpart and required fewer calories.

In one Formosan prison camp, prisoners received two-thirds of a cup of rice and a bowl of vegetable soup for breakfast, lunch, and dinner every day. At Zentsuji, Commander Giles usually received three meals per day, although this fluctuated as the war dragged on. A breakfast of tea and *lugao*, a watery rice gruel, was followed by a lunch and dinner of rice, pickled or steamed seaweed, and tea. Prisoners occasionally created a soup, called *benjo*, by boiling fish heads with potato vines, leaves, and other greens. "Meat was never seen," stated Giles, "nor was any form of seafood, except for the occasional fish head that found its way into the *benjo* soup."[41]

The Red Cross

Prisoners supplemented their meager diets in various ways. The most common was the Red Cross parcel. Each prisoner of war was supposed to receive one each week, plus an additional parcel from home every two months. Few ever saw the proper ration, however, and in the Pacific there was an almost criminal withholding of these packages by Japanese authorities. The parcels contained food, cigarettes, and other amenities designed to ease life for prisoners of war, as well as clothing and medical supplies.

German guards inspected each Red Cross parcel to remove any item they thought could be used against them. For in-

---

Red Cross Parcel

Though the contents of a typical Red Cross parcel varied depending upon which nation packaged it, it contained many items that helped prisoners of war survive. The boost to morale was, in itself, sufficient to justify the parcel, but the food and sundry items proved invaluable. In his book about American prisoners of war, *Surrender and Survival: The Experience of American POWs in the Pacific, 1941–1945*, E. Bartlett Kerr describes what a prisoner might find in his package, depending upon what the guards took.

Evaporated milk	one 14.5-ounce can
Lunch biscuits	one 8-ounce package
Cheese	one 8-ounce package
Instant cocoa	one 8-ounce tin
Sardines	one 15-ounce tin
Oleomargarine	one 1-pound tin
Corned beef	one 12-ounce tin
Sweet chocolate	two 5.5-ounce bars
Sugar	one 2-ounce package
Powdered orange concentrate	two 3.5-ounce packages
Dehydrated soup	two 2.5-ounce packages
Prunes	one 16-ounce package
Instant coffee	one 4-ounce tin
Cigarettes	one package of 10
Smoking tobacco	one 2.25-ounce package

stance, pepper was confiscated because Germans feared the spice would be tossed into guard dogs' eyes. Guards also punctured each can of food to prevent prisoners from accumulating large amounts of food that could be later used during escape attempts.

German officials generally refrained from stealing any of the items for their own use until late in the war, when supplies were harder to obtain. German guards were even known to hand out Red Cross supplies, then trade other items with prisoners for their cigarettes.

On occasions such as Christmas or New Year's Day the prisoners received untampered parcels. However, camp doctors cautioned them to avoid eating too much, since their bodies had become unaccustomed to such rich fare. Not surprisingly, most warnings went unheeded by the famished prisoners.

Except for chocolate bars, cigarettes, and jam, which everyone agreed should be retained by the recipient, most men helped one another by pooling other supplies from Red Cross parcels and packages from home.

As the war wound down in its final year, 1945, Red Cross parcels and packages from home dwindled to a trickle or stopped altogether. Captain Vietor stated that "although we thought we had been hungry before, we didn't know the meaning of the word until then." With their bread ration and potatoes at Stalag Luft I reduced, and items such as

Red Cross parcels are prepared for shipment. Prison camp guards often tampered with the packages or withheld them from prisoners.

barley totally eliminated, men hoarded what precious amounts of food they could get. "We watched each other like vultures around the table," added Vietor, "absurdly jealous that one might have more than the other." Vietor concluded that "at best the lack of food made men despondent and irritable; at worst, chiseling and greedy."[42] As a partial solution men began eating the camp's cats, but that backfired when the rat population skyrocketed.

American prisoners languishing in Japanese camps would have been delighted to receive as many Red Cross packages as their cohorts in Europe. Though seized in 1941, Commander Giles did not see a Red Cross parcel until 1943, and during his entire incarceration he received no more than eight bundles. Each package had been opened, items pilfered (especially cigarettes and chocolate bars), and only moldy or stale foodstuffs remained. Sometimes men stared across camp at a building in which the Japanese stored the Red Cross parcels, tormented by the knowledge that much-needed food rested barely out of arm's reach.

Other Ways to Obtain Food

In the midst of misery, prisoners in both German and Japanese camps found ways to improve their lives. Since the Geneva Convention required that the men receive wages (about thirty-eight dollars per month) for their work, many Japanese and German camps opened stores where prisoners could purchase a few supplies. Camps established a bartering system in which prisoners could trade items and listed the exchange rate on bulletin boards. At Stalag Luft I, twenty cigarettes might bring a loaf of bread, but one needed two hundred or more to get highly prized chocolate.

In Japanese camps, Commander Giles and others enjoyed the opportunity to pick up something extra. "We couldn't obtain edibles, which was what we wanted more than anything else," but the men could browse through a stack of old records, some pencils, paper, ink, and pens. Though it may not have appeared to be much, "it proved to be another morale-boosting activity, as we had hoped. Just being able to look at what was there was a tonic for many of us."[43] The camp at Cabanatuan in the Philippines of-

fered coffee, eggs, chickens, vegetables, and fruit to the men fortunate enough to have some money.

Prisoners who labored on German farms normally could steal an egg or two, or even receive a chicken from a friendly farmer. They smuggled the food back into camp, where most shared the bounty with their blockmates.

Americans sometimes obtained products from German guards. Sergeant William C. Bradley, confined at Stalag IIIA, said, "We could get the German guards to do anything for American cigarettes. You could have gotten a free trip across Berlin if you'd wanted it. But I traded cigarettes with them and they would turn their heads long enough for me to sneak out of the compound and over to an Italian camp, where I could get food."[44]

Prisoners levied a heavy punishment on anyone who tried to steal from a fellow inmate. Sergeant Bradley recalled that at Stalag IIIA, one prisoner stole another American's cigarettes. "This is one thing that you didn't do—you could steal from the Germans, but not from your buddies."[45] The men in his barracks put the man on trial, found him guilty, and sentenced him to fight the camp's boxing champion. After he was mauled by the champion, the men placed a sign around his neck proclaiming, "I am a thief. I stole from my buddies," and marched him about the entire camp.

Others employed various tricks to smuggle in food while they were on jobs which took them outside the camp. Men in one

In a scene from Stalag 17, *a film about a German POW camp, a prisoner attempts to bribe a guard with American cigarettes.*

At Cabanatuan, Private First Class Michael Tussig joined the others in eating whatever they could find.

We got rice so full of weevils that it looked like it had been heavily sprinkled with black pepper. You ate the weevils, too, thinking there might be some vitamins in them. And there were worms, little white ones with brownish heads. I can still see their eyes. If you'd have picked them out, there wouldn't have been anything left.[47]

Japanese warehouse surreptitiously crept toward bags of salt, sugar, or wheat, slit open the bags, then let the pouring material flow down their pant legs, which they had knotted at the cuff.

All prisoners learned that if they wanted to survive, they had to be willing to eat anything, even watery soup or insect-laden rice. Giles claimed that "Anything that crawled contained some of the protein that we so greatly lacked, and we convinced ourselves that many low forms of life were delicious."[46]

In the Philippines, Americans set up an arrangement with willing guards. The prisoners lined up near a guard's tower and threw money to him. The guard tossed down a rope to a waiting Filipino on the outside, who attached a basket containing bananas, candy, molasses, or mangoes. The guard gave a portion of the money to the Filipino, pocketed the rest, and the Americans returned to the barracks with the food.

In all camps, the prisoners tried in some way, no matter how small, to duplicate the lives they lived back home. This led to an astonishing array of physical contests, entertainment activities, and methods of communication.

Chapter 4

"Would Things Ever Get Better?"

Even in prison camp, Americans found ways to lighten their moods and diminish the mental and physical pain they endured. By keeping their thoughts away from the unpleasant realities of everyday life behind barbed wire, the different camp diversions improved morale. Information from home, camp newspapers, sporting and entertainment events, and educational programs helped pull men through trying ordeals.

Rumors

When people find themselves in dire predicaments, they frequently hold onto thoughts, even if outlandish, that lighten the situation. Rumors swirled about most camps, especially early in the war, that created momentary optimism among the prisoners. Commander Donald Giles and the other men confined at Zentsuji assumed in 1942 that "in Hollywood style, the U.S. fleet would come barreling over the horizon with guns blazing and relieve us."[48]

When that did not occur, the men believed that the fleet did not appear because it was busy fighting the Japanese elsewhere. They did not know of the disastrous string of defeats suffered by American forces in early 1942, and, even if word filtered in about the calamities, for self-protection they would have to doubt their accuracy. As Giles wrote, "I can say that there was merit in the old saying, 'Ignorance is bliss.' Had we known of the extent of our losses, I am not certain that we could have hung on at Zentsuji. Perhaps it was better to fool ourselves, and to receive the bad news in dribs and drabs."[49]

Corporal Kenneth Day was able to wake up each morning at Davao prison camp in the Philippines because of the hope offered by rumors.

We had thirty-, sixty-, and ninety-day rumors assuring us that the war would be over within that time. Many men lived on these dated projections. Those who believed them were not

Early in the war, American prisoners in the Pacific believed that the U.S. fleet would come to their rescue. They did not know that much of the fleet had been sunk or damaged at Pearl Harbor (pictured).

camp, claimed that "We were sure Uncle Sam was coming after us. It was just a matter of how soon." He added, "To say that many of our men actually kept alive on these hopes is no exaggeration."[51]

In Europe, rumors asserted that a ship was being painted white and would be used to ship men home, that the United States had agreed to peace, that POWs would be transferred to a neutral nation and confined there until war's end, and that automotive pioneer Henry Ford planned to give each returning prisoner of war a new car. A common rumor contended that the war would be over by Christmas, and when that did not occur, the rumor simply started over again for the next Christmas.

Not all rumors were beneficial. Private First Class George J. Davis, interned at Stalag IVB in Germany, heard with dismay that

disheartened when they failed to come true; they would just latch onto the next rumor and ride it out.[50]

Lieutenant Colonel William E. Dyess, who later escaped from his Japanese prison

all of us would be court-martialed after the war for allowing ourselves to be captured. . . . We thought we were losing our home support, and quite naturally, a lot of us felt terribly depressed that something like this might happen. After all, we had almost been killed in battle, after which we had to suffer those long months as guests of the Germans. Certainly we didn't choose to become prisoners.[52]

Mail

One of the most frustrating aspects of camp life was the complete unpredictability of sending and receiving mail. Prisoners never knew when, if ever, letters from home would be delivered, and they could not count on their letters being delivered to parents or loved ones. Most Japanese commandants periodically permitted the prisoners to send cards on which they could write no more than twenty-five to fifty words. This allowed them to include little more than brief greetings. If the card left camp, it might take a year or more to reach the United States.

German authorities handled the issue more leniently, but even in Europe no one could count on regular delivery. Prisoners could send four letters and three postcards each month, which captive officers censored to guarantee that nothing could be used in German propaganda.

Some prisoners experienced great emotional stress while waiting for word from home, especially if they had to watch other prisoners open mail. One man received a weekly letter from home for over two years.

POWs stroll the grounds of a Stalag. Rumors circulating in prison camps brought both hope and despair to those held captive.

Another prisoner received thirty-six letters at one time, all written on different dates. Sometimes letters arrived bearing postmarks from only two weeks before, while others carried postmarks up to a year old. One prisoner in a German camp received two letters from his wife on the same day, one dated March 1943 and the other dated March 1945. In the Pacific, General Jonathan Wainwright, who had commanded all American forces in the Philippines before the surrender, received six letters from his wife during his more than three years in captivity. Mrs. Wainwright had written over three hundred.

A wife writes to her husband, a POW. Delivery of mail to prisoners was sporadic, and sometimes the news from home was not good.

While prisoners happily devoured most mail, some letters were better undelivered. A surprisingly large number of wives and girlfriends wrote notes indicating the romance was off. Captain Vietor explained that "it was distressing how many wives were unfaithful and wrote their prisoner husbands to that effect."[53] Already demoralized by camp conditions, these men often became depressed—some never recovered.

Other sentiments from home could negatively affect the prisoners, particularly if the letters mentioned the POW's surrender. Prisoners were sensitive to charges that they had given up too quickly or that they had shamed the military, especially when they read such sentiments from home. One man ripped open a letter from his wife which stated, "I still love you even if you are a coward and a prisoner."[54]

Radio Broadcasts

Most camps in both Europe and the Pacific contained radio receivers that had been smuggled into the camp by prisoners or made from scavenged parts. Americans hid radios in musical instruments, under floorboards, or anywhere that provided a safe location from German and Japanese authorities, who considered possession of such an item one of the worst infractions.

Most secret radios in German camps tuned in to a nightly BBC broadcast sent by the British government from London, England. Prisoners trusted this source of information and thus had some idea of recent events. A small group of prisoners listened to the news, wrote it down, made handwritten copies, and distributed them to other barracks. The daily sheet of news was read in every room and then destroyed.

A second source of information, though far less reliable, came from German and Japanese propaganda broadcasts. The Germans placed loudspeakers in each barracks at Stalag Luft I and piped in radio programs from Berlin. While the prisoners realized they were being fed doctored news, they enjoyed listening to the outrageous remarks made by German commentators and appreciated the infrequent music.

An American-born Japanese named Uno supervised a daily radio broadcast from Japan titled *Humanity Calls*, which consisted of propaganda statements interspersed with American POWs speaking to people back home. While prisoners dismissed the propaganda, at least information about captives reached loved ones in the United States. Shortwave radio operators along the American West Coast picked up the broadcasts and relayed the material to families.

Newspapers

Prisoners communicated news and other items through camp newspapers, although these were heavily censored by camp authorities. Stalag Luft I put out a daily newspaper which included information from freshly arrived prisoners and a comic strip about a POW who constantly tried to escape.

The Germans assembled an English-language newspaper for prison camps called *O.K.*, which stood for "Overseas Kid." The publication included editorials, comics, and news that cast the United States in a negative light. Murders, Hollywood divorces, industrial strikes, and setbacks in the Pacific filled the paper's pages. Prisoners realized what they were getting, but as John Vietor wrote, "the papers were avidly read before being consigned to a more valuable function in the latrine [as toilet paper]." [55]

Some camps in the Pacific received English-language versions of Japanese newspapers. It did not take prisoners long to determine that reports of American losses were greatly exaggerated. For instance, they frequently read that Japanese naval forces sank numerous American ships without losing one of their own, and they noticed that the same American ship was reported as sunk in more than one engagement.

Without any way to verify information, men battled with the disturbing idea that the United States might be losing the conflict, especially in 1942 and 1943 when the Japanese rolled to victory after victory. Commander Giles wrote of those early months, "All of the news was so bad. We felt as though we were being slowly but surely pounded into the ground. Would things ever get better?" [56] However, prisoners in Japanese camps figured that the war had turned in the United States' favor when fewer reports of military action appeared in the papers.

Sports

With free time on their hands, prisoners in many camps established sporting events. They formed teams and leagues, and fellow prisoners cheered their comrades to victory along the sidelines. The Red Cross sent equipment to prison camps, such as baseballs, bats, and footballs, but whether the prisoners received the items depended, as always, upon the whim of the camp commandant.

Since many camps housed prisoners from different nations, the men organized contests which pitted nation against nation. The men played not only for exercise and to pass the time but also for the honor of their nations. The games gave purpose to the

Two prisoners compete in a boxing match. Sporting events helped ease the burden of captivity by giving purpose to prisoners' time in camp.

POWs' time in camp and provided a connection with their homelands. Like soldiers in the field, they battled on behalf of their countries.

In order to have more competition at Stalag Luft I, British prisoners learned to play American baseball. In turn, American prisoners studied the basics of one of England's favorite sports and organized a rugby team. A flurry of bets surrounded the matches, as prisoners hoped to gain extra food, cigarettes, or other items.

Even in a sporting activity the men received reminders that they were captives. Lieutenant Paul H. Smith, imprisoned at Stalag XIIA, recalled that "if we were playing baseball, we didn't dare go toward the fence [surrounding camp]. If the ball got loose and went toward the fence, you'd better make sure a guard in the tower knew it. You'd have to yell at him and point to the ball. He'd let you go get it, but all the while you were near the fence, he'd have a rifle pointed at you."[57]

At Stalag Luft I Captain Vietor and the others received a shipment of ice skates from the Red Cross. At first they started to convert them into weapons, but when the Germans caught on, the prisoners agreed to use the skates on parole—which meant they would not try to escape or alter the skates for use in escape attempts. From then on the skates were used only for recreation.

The Americans at Zentsuji did not enjoy the luxury of athletic equipment like Vietor and the others in Europe. Even if they received the items, most camps had no space large enough for team sports. That did not stop a group at one camp from enjoying a relaxing afternoon of baseball, however. Commander Donald Giles explains,

> One day we organized an entire game on the road beside our barracks. A pitcher would pitch a nonexistent ball, and a batter would pretend to hit it. Bases were run, and a slide was made at home plate: SAFE! The Japanese guards who watched were flabbergasted.[58]

Arts and Crafts

Besides sporting events, prisoners of war in Europe and the Philippines lightened their time in captivity with periodic dramatic and musical performances. Some camps formed glee clubs to entertain the men, while others built elaborate sets and staged plays. According to John Vietor, "We had sufficient musical instruments to have both a symphony and a swing band." He added that "it is impossible to underestimate the psychological value of the entertainment facilities. They made life bearable for many a lonesome Kriegie [prisoner]."[59]

One officer at Zentsuji formed a group called the Bathhouse Gang. Members performed popular American tunes such as "Penny Serenade," "Tuxedo Junction," "In the Mood," and almost eighty other tunes.

Prisoners at Cabanatuan in the Philippines added a seriousness and a professional air to their performances. Band concerts were held most Wednesdays, and a

Two POWs perform in a makeshift concert. Some prison camps established complete symphony orchestras and swing bands.

stage play or musical occurred on Saturdays. The camp orchestra, the Cabanatuan Cats, imitated the leading big bands, such as Glenn Miller. Their Mighty Art Players performed *Gone with the Wind* and *Frankenstein.*

Some of the performances included comedy, which Giles said "brought laughter from men who had almost forgotten how to laugh." In the presence of a Japanese interpreter, who carefully listened to the skits to ensure the prisoners were not making fun of the Japanese, the prisoners temporarily left their miserable surroundings and felt as though they were once again back home. "Tales were told, many songs sung, pantomimes performed, and poems recited.

Thus, for an hour or more each week devotees of the stage whisked fellow prisoners out of the doldrums and into another world. The roars of laughter and sustained applause were medicine for all."[60]

Most camps offered some form of education to the prisoners, ranging from casual gatherings to structured classes. One camp held lectures in each block on a wide variety of topics. Men at Zentsuji opened what they

In many camps, prisoners could pass the time by attending lectures given by fellow POWs. Here, men file into a classroom that has been set up in a Stalag.

and records to the prisoners at Zentsuji. Eventually, their library contained more than five hundred volumes.

Libraries contained the works of William Shakespeare, Charles Dickens, and Mark Twain. German authorities allowed mysteries, philosophy, and theology but forbade history volumes because they worried that the factual writing might contain critical interpretations of the German people. Many prisoners took advantage of spare time to lose themselves in a piece of fiction or a biography. In his stay at Stalag Luft I, Captain Vietor read 212 books.

Army Air Corps Lieutenant Nicholas Katzenbach established an arduous eight-hour-a-day reading regimen at Stalag Luft III, and in two years he read over four hundred books on politics, economics, and literature. Following the war, Princeton University allowed Katzenbach to take the course examinations and write the required papers without attending classes. Katzenbach graduated and went on to a distinguished political career that included becoming the U.S. Attorney General.

Men created other diversions to occupy free moments and to get their minds off their confinement. Card games, including poker and bridge, were popular, although little gambling occurred because most men hated to part

called Zentsuji College. Commander Donald Giles, who had a background in mechanical engineering, offered a course in engineering. Another prisoner, who had graduated from the Harvard Business School, taught business and administration, and an oilman taught petroleum engineering and sales engineering. Other classes included foreign languages, history, law, and psychology.

Many prison camps collected a camp library. Men could check out one book each week from volumes provided by the Red Cross or sent over from families back home. When the U.S. ambassador to Japan, Joseph C. Grew, had to leave Japan early in the war, he donated his personal collection of books with their cigarettes or chocolate. Men entered bridge or chess tournaments, while others constructed model airplanes from wood and even model homes from barley. One man in a Japanese camp scavenged for spare automobile parts until he finally assembled a Ford Model A engine.

Escape

The image of hundreds of prisoners of war escaping and returning to their own forces is more a creation of television and Hollywood than reality. While Americans participated in escape attempts, less than 1 percent actually succeeded. Of the 121,000 American prisoners of war captured by the Germans from 1942–1945, only 737 escaped.

Many decided not even to make the effort. The obstacles appeared too difficult to surmount. Should a prisoner break out of camp, he still had to travel hundreds of miles across enemy-controlled territory before reaching his own troops. Everyone knew that an escape attempt usually brought harsher rules on those who remained in camp, so if one evaded security and headed into the countryside, he did so knowing that he may have made things worse for his buddies.

Most Americans in Europe were captured in the war's final year, when victory over German forces appeared certain. Since prisoners believed that they would soon be freed,

they had little reason to risk their lives in an escape attempt. The American armed forces made steady advances across France on their way toward Germany, and few prisoners saw the necessity of organizing a breakout. They could wait because soon their own troops would crash through the barbed wire.

An American fighting vehicle passes through Paris, France. As U.S. forces advanced toward Germany, many prisoners felt little need for escape attempts.

David Westheimer, who later wrote the script for a movie about prisoners of war titled *Von Ryan's Express*, explained why he chose not to escape, even when a guard fell asleep one time and let his rifle fall out of his hands.

Grumpily I leaned it back in place and dozed off. It fell on me again. This time it occurred to me we could easily disarm our guards and escape. I didn't even consider it. Like most veteran prisoners, I'd have loved to escape if it were handed to me on a platter but when it came to planning one I found the obstacles daunting. . . . I didn't know where I was except that it was deep in enemy territory with no underground [friendly civilians] to help me, it was too cold to exist for long in open country, I was in the wrong uniform, and my German would never fool anyone. Maybe most important, when I was picked up, as I certainly would be, I'd have lost all the food and clothing I'd accumulated so painstakingly over the long months.[61]

Escape Committees

In spite of the small numbers who successfully escaped, most American prisoners of war either helped plan escapes or contributed skills to the undertaking in some way. They realized that those who broke out might not reach American lines, but while they were on the loose they would tie up large numbers of enemy soldiers who would normally be fighting in the front lines or carrying out regular military duties.

"There are a lot of criminals you just can't keep in prison," said prisoner of war Sergeant Ernest de los Santos. "They'd rather be dead than spend their lives behind bars. I can understand that. I was always trying to escape. I'm not sure why. Even before I went in the service, I just couldn't stay put. I used to hitchhike everywhere."[62] Though de los Santos tried many times to escape, he never evaded the Germans for more than a few days.

A Successful Escape

Though few men broke out of prison camp and safely returned to their own lines, a handful did accomplish the feat. Lieutenant Paul H. Smith fled Stalag XIIA in October 1944. He recounts his adventure in Harry Spiller's book, *Prisoners of Nazis: Accounts by American POWs in World War II*.

One day we were working near some timber. As soon as the guards were looking the other way, I slipped into the timber and ran. I ran till I dropped.

You know, if someone is crazy, you don't like to be around them. Every town has their town drunk or town idiot, and nobody wants to associate with them. So when I got out of camp, I just acted like I was crazy. Some people would yell at me, trying to find out who I was, but I would just wave at them and keep walking.

Smith eventually met friendly troops, and on December 26, 1944, he boarded a ship headed for the United States.

Each POW camp in Germany organized a committee to coordinate all plans for escape. No prisoner was supposed to attempt a breakout without the committee's approval, and to earn its endorsement the POW would have to present a thorough plan. If the committee agreed that the escape held a chance of success, it placed all its resources at his disposal. Inmates forged documents, made German uniforms, and traded or bribed guards for German money so the soldier stood a chance of evading detection. At the moment of the breakout, the committee made sure to hold a boxing match or other sporting event to divert attention.

The most efficient escape committee in Germany was at Stalag Luft III, southeast of Berlin. In two years the prisoners set up a superb mapmaking division, enlisted former tailors to make clothes, and dug over one hundred tunnels. They even had their own nutritionist who designed a calorie-laden snack that escapees could take with them. A four-ounce mixture of oatmeal, chocolate, sugar, raisins, and other high-energy foods, baked to a hardened consistency, the item contained sufficient calories to sustain a man for at least two days.

Though Americans tried different methods to escape, tunneling proved to be the most popular because a group of men could squeeze underground and exit through an opening on the other side of the fence. The activity also unified the camp in a common endeavor. Tunneling required a vast amount of work. Enormous amounts of dirt had to be removed from the tunnel and dispersed throughout the camp. The endeavor could only succeed if everyone pitched in.

Men climbed over fences, cut through the barbed wire, or ran into forests while working on details outside the camp. One soldier sewed hundreds of tin cans onto a uniform, then hid in a truck that removed empty cans from the camp. He blended into his hiding place enough to make it out the gate, but guard dogs discovered him shortly after.

Another inmate vaulted over a ten-foot barbed wire fence and ran away. When German soldiers caught him later that evening and returned him to camp, the commandant refused to believe that the American had jumped such a tall obstacle. He told the prisoner that he would not punish him if he could again jump the fence, and when the prisoner easily repeated the vault, the commandant ordered the fences heightened.

The most famous escape of World War II occurred on March 24, 1944, when seventy-six British and American officers broke out of Stalag Luft III at Sagan. An enraged Hitler ordered all available troops to hunt down the prisoners. Though most were caught within fifty miles of camp, three British officers managed to escape. The German secret police, the Gestapo, machine-gunned fifty escapees on Hitler's orders.

Escape from Pacific prison camps proved nearly impossible. At least in Germany many POWs looked like their captors, but in the Pacific the men had no hope of

Tunneling Out of Camp

One of the most heralded escape attempts in war occurred in March 1944 in what is called the "Great Escape" from Stalag Luft III at Sagan. To achieve this breakout, the prisoners dug three tunnels thirty feet deep and at least three hundred feet long. In his history, *Prisoners of War*, Ronald H. Bailey describes some of the amazing features of the tunnels, nicknamed Tom, Dick, and Harry.

Tom, Dick and Harry were lighted by stolen bulbs and wiring tapped into the camp's electrical system. Sand from the face of the tunnels was carried back on wooden trolleys pulled by rope along wooden rails. Later, the trolleys would speed the movement of escape. The tunnels even had ventilation. Air pumps resembling bellows were improvised from canvas kit bags fitted around wooden frames and equipped with valves; conduit pipes were made of powdered-milk cans taped together.

In a scene from the movie The Great Escape, *two POWs tunnel out of their German prison camp.*

blending in. Besides, dense jungle surrounded many camps, or the camps were in Japan itself, where escape was futile.

Even in the Pacific, however, some tried. The most renowned attempt occurred in 1943 when three American officers who had survived the Bataan Death March, including William E. Dyess, escaped from their prison camp in the Philippines, fled into the jungle, and, with the aid of friendly Filipino forces, eventually made radio contact with American authorities in Australia. A submarine arranged to extricate the three from the Philippines.

When Dyess returned to the United States, he wrote a report which included the grisly details of the Death March and horrendous treatment inside Japanese prison camps. The American public and politicians were outraged that the Japanese would treat human beings so brutally, and they wondered what the fate of other prisoners might be.

While many fellow prisoners cheered the success of the trio, others chafed under severe Japanese reprisals. The remaining prisoners had to work longer hours, endure more frequent searches, and had their food supply further limited.

Steps to Prevent Escape

Both German and Japanese authorities took measures to safeguard against breakouts. Germans built barracks on pilings which raised the floor above the ground and made escape attempts easier to detect. A double barrier of barbed wire enclosed each camp, and guard towers with searchlights and guards with machine guns commanded a view of every corner in camp.

A warning line marked the farthest a prisoner could safely walk; one step beyond could mean quick death by machine gun bullet. Dogs and guards patrolled inside and outside of camp, commandants made sur-

prise inspections, and authorities planted microphones into the soil to pick up noises caused by tunnel digging.

Severe punishment was handed out to anyone who attempted to escape. In Germany, any prisoner caught outside the camp barricade could expect either a beating or two weeks in solitary confinement with little food or water. Yet the Germans respected that a prisoner of war's duty was to escape.

The Japanese did not respond to escape attempts with similar understanding. Since they thought that a prisoner had disgraced himself and his army, Japanese retribution was quick and harsh for any prisoner unfortunate enough to be recaptured. If the man was not instantly executed, he could expect prolonged beatings and lack of food.

The Japanese tried to forestall escape attempts by organizing prisoners into groups of ten men. If one man escaped, the other nine would be shot, so few prisoners thought escaping worthwhile. After one escape from a Philippine camp, the Japanese lined up the nine men from the escapee's group and, with the entire camp forced to watch, executed them. One twin had to watch his twin brother die because they had been placed in different groups.

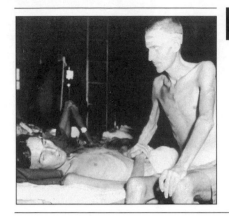

Chapter 5

"A War of Wills"

For American prisoners in both German and Japanese prison camps, life boiled down to a daily struggle to endure hardships and stay alive. Although the men engaged in different activities and responded in various ways, little else entered the equation except making it through one day and surviving until the next.

The commander of the marines captured on Wake Island, Major James Devereux, said after the war,

Hidden behind the routine, under the surface of life in prison camp, was fought a war of wills for moral supremacy—an endless struggle, as bitter as it was unspoken, between the captors and the captives. The stakes seemed to be simply this: The main objective of the whole Japanese prison program was to break our spirit, and on our side was a stubborn determination to keep our self-respect whatever else they took from us. It seems to me that struggle was almost as much a part of the War [sic] as the battle we fought on Wake Island.[63]

The Ordeals of a Japanese Prison Camp

"Reality for us was the lack of food, the lack of medical care, the physical labor, the increasingly frequent beatings, and the gradual loss of hope,"[64] explained Commander Donald Giles of his time at Zentsuji. His experience was typical for POWs in Japanese camps. Infractions such as being too slow or forgetting to bow to a Japanese soldier resulted in a severe beating with a bamboo stick, water from a hose being forced down the prisoner's throat, or being made to kneel with a bamboo stick behind the knees. In one Japanese camp, if an American broke a dish he had to write a letter begging forgiveness, then stand outside at attention and hold the broken pieces at arm's length for an hour or more, even in freezing weather.

After liberation, two American officers demonstrate how their Japanese captors treated them. Even the simplest violation of the rules could result in a beating.

Many men endured the tortures as a part of their harsh existence. Some even used it to spur their determination to survive. A few, however, lost their sanity.

Those guards who seemed to relish punishing the captives earned nicknames from the American prisoners. "The Beast of the East" tormented Americans in a camp near Shanghai, while a man called the "Mad Monk" on the Celebes administered punishment on a daily basis.

Though not as common in the Pacific as in Europe, American prisoners baited guards whenever opportunity offered. The consequences, however, could be severe. Corporal Bernard Saunders recalled that everyone at Cabanatuan called one guard Donald Duck. "We all told him he was a famous Hollywood movie star. The Jap thought that was fine and would strut around thinking he looked like a famous star. In Manila one day he happened to catch a Disney cartoon. When he got back to camp, he beat the hell out of everybody for weeks."[65]

In all prison compounds, more Americans died from disease, illness, and malnutrition than from torture. This was particularly so in Japanese camps, where almost four out of every ten prisoners died. The death rate in German camps was less than 4 percent.

Besides the punishment of the guards, Americans in the Pacific battled a deadly array of exotic diseases. A condition called beriberi, caused by lack of vitamins, produced swelling throughout the body and brought excruciating pain. Other vitamin deficiencies such as pellagra and scurvy, which attack the digestive system and the brain, so weakened men that they lan-

At the end of the war, prisoners freed from a Japanese camp await medical treatment for injuries suffered during captivity.

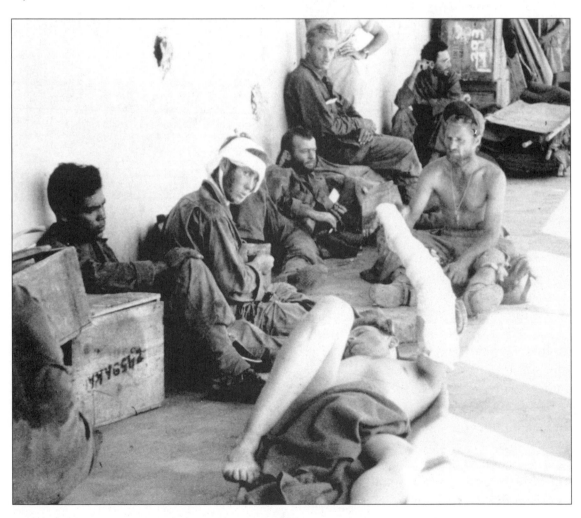

Zero Ward

Camp Cabanatuan in the Philippines, like most camps under Japanese supervision, had a building to which the most seriously ill men were taken. The building housed misery and anguish for patients and doctors alike. Major Roy L. Bodine, a dental officer, explains Zero Ward in the book by E. Bartlett Kerr, *Surrender and Survival: The Experience of American POWs in the Pacific, 1941–1945*:

> The men were nearly all naked, having soiled and thrown away their clothing and blanket, as there were no means to wash them and no one to do it. The one doctor assigned to watch each building could do nothing for his patients except try to encourage them as he watched them die; the two medical corps men [sic] assigned were busy trying to distribute evenly the meager amounts of water and food. Once each day the helpless, bedsore human skeletons were moved from their own filth so a crude attempt could be made to scrape and sweep the mess to one end of the building. A haze of giant green flies covered the area and crawled over the eyes and in and out of the mouths of the dying men.

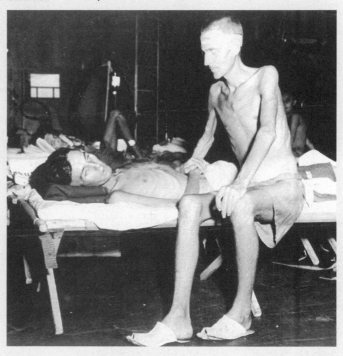

A POW comforts a dying comrade in a camp hospital.

guished in sick wards with barely sufficient strength to remain alive. Malaria, so common in Asian lands, produced dangerously high body temperatures and mind-numbing chills, while a severe form of diarrhea, called dysentery, drained every ounce of strength from the prisoners. Malaria and dysentery killed more American POWs than any other illnesses.

Most camps in the Pacific designated one structure as the place in which the dying men spent their final hours. The men of one camp in the Philippines labeled it the "Zero Ward" because no man who entered ever left alive, while Camp O'Donnell in the Philippines had its "St. Peter's Ward." The huge volume of deathly ill prisoners swamped the meager facilities available to the overworked American military physicians.

In the makeshift Japanese hospitals, men lay in their own filth, too weak to budge. Many suffered a slow, painful death far from loved ones. One prisoner explained, "A man should have a bit of dignity for himself, even in death. But that's what we haven't got."[66]

The presence of death hovered over entire camps, affecting moods and willpower. William Wallace, a private interned at a camp in Japan, said,

> Everyone came close to dying, so as Mr. Darwin said, it became survival of the fittest. In my camp the biggest and healthiest took the easiest jobs. . . . At the end there was very little decency or human dignity left. Humanity had long since departed from camp. Human worth had disappeared. We were just animals and that's all it amounted to.[67]

Since there was not enough quinine to treat all the malaria cases that appeared in the jungle-rimmed camp, doctors at Camp O'Donnell had to decide which men received the lifesaving drug. In some cases, the medical staff used a lottery to select the fortunate patients. In spite of the physicians' efforts, almost one in every six men died from disease at Camp O'Donnell.

Those who survived Japanese camps shrank to a shadow of their former selves. Walking skeletons emerged from the war with a variety of afflictions. Staff Sergeant James Cavanaugh, imprisoned at Kawasaki, explained, "At the end I weighed 120 pounds, soaking wet. If you bent over, it would take half a minute to straighten out. You'd make all kinds of funny noises as your bones creaked."[68]

The Ordeals of A German Prison Camp

While prisoners in Japanese camps stared death in the face every day, men in German camps existed in less threatening conditions. The "Kriegies," as American prisoners in German camps called themselves (after the German word *Kriegsgefangenen*), engaged in activities they labeled "fouling up the goons." This seemingly endless parade of actions had a sole purpose—to make life miserable for the German guards.

Prisoners at one German camp tossed snowballs at a guard with poor eyesight because they knew he could not identify them. In another camp, German guards regularly spied on American POWs by crawling underneath the barracks' floor. Americans waited while the guards slid beneath the barracks, then engaged in fictional discussions about a secret weapon the Americans possessed, or chatted about plans for an upcoming invasion. Captain John Vietor later wrote:

> After we had given them the best misinformation we could, we took pots of boiling water and poured it in the cracks of the floor above where we

heard rustling. When we heard the scuttling of the scorched guards our evening's entertainment was ended.[69]

Prisoners of war could engage in these activities because most German soldiers understood that the prisoners were doing their best to make life harder for their captors, something they would do if the situation was reversed. Americans in Japanese camps could not be so blatant in taunting their guards, who would usually react with anger and extreme cruelty.

Men in German camps endured spending time in what they termed the "hole," a cell too small even to lie down in. Depending upon the severity of their "crime,"

the men spent a week or more in this solitary confinement, subsisting on a single piece of bread and a glass of water each day. Infractions calling for a stint in the hole ranged from being late for roll call to attempting to escape.

Camp Inspections

According to the Geneva Convention, the International Red Cross had the right to inspect camps to ensure that the prisoners were properly treated. As with everything else pertaining to the rights of prisoners, Germany and Japan followed the convention only when it suited them, especially Japan, which had not signed the Geneva Convention. The inspections occurred infrequently, and only in camps carefully selected by the Germans or Japanese. Representatives from the Red Cross were allowed to visit a handful of camps in Japan, but no team received permission to enter prison camps in the Philippines or other Pacific locales, where conditions were shocking. At Zentsuji, the prisoners had to clean the camp before the Red Cross team arrived so they would find conditions acceptable. Giles wrote that "we were worked extremely hard to make what was actually a lousy camp appear presentable."[70]

The visits lasted no longer than a few hours, and camp authorities carefully guided the team around so it would see only what they wanted the team to observe. Normally, the team met for one hour with the camp commandant, visited barracks for thirty minutes, and spent another half hour

Teasing the Guards

One pastime many Americans in German camps engaged in was playing tricks on the guards. Though they had to be careful not to push too far, Americans enjoyed brief moments of laughter that helped brighten a dismal day. In the book by Lewis H. Carlson, *We Were Each Other's Prisoners*, Philip Miller relates an example of teasing a guard.

We drove this one guard practically mad. He marched very stiffly so the prisoners began to count cadence: "Hup, two, three, four." And just as he reached the gate everyone would holler, "Halt!" He tolerated this for awhile but began growing noticeably more angry. He tried speeding up his steps, but the count speeded up with him. He slowed down, but so did the count. He stopped and faced the crowd, and the crowd stopped. He started up again, and the count went right along with him.

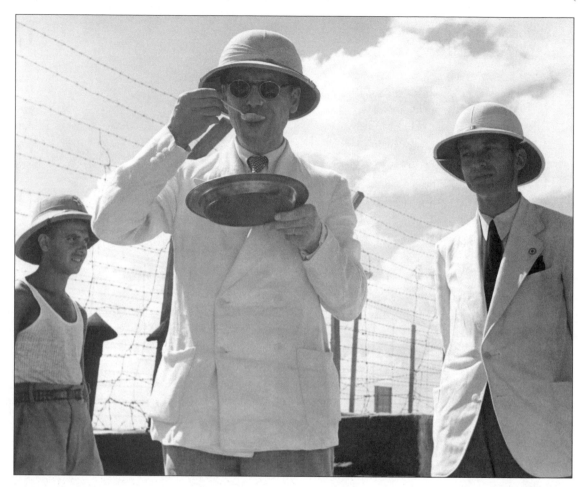

A Red Cross representative samples the food at a prison camp in Japan. Due to their inhumane living conditions, camps in the Philippines and other Pacific areas were kept off-limits to Red Cross inspections.

talking to the senior POW officer. Since Japanese or German officers accompanied the teams, prisoners knew they could not freely criticize their captors without expecting to be severely punished afterward.

While the visits did not benefit the Americans, they did provide information for families back home. The American Red Cross printed news of the inspections, names of prisoners, and whatever else they uncovered in the *Prisoner of War Bulletin* and mailed it to relatives. This welcome newsletter at least let parents and wives know that their loved ones were alive.

Mental Games

One of the most difficult aspects of prison life was coping with the mental hardships. Loneliness, boredom, anger, depression, frustration, and a host of other emotions assaulted each prisoner. The manner in which a prisoner handled these feelings at times meant the difference between life and death. Private George J. Davis explained of his time at Stalag IVB, "Individually and collectively, we were humbled by our loss of freedom, our inability to influence events in our daily lives, and by our ignorance of events that were determining the outcome of the war." [71]

Most men later said that the worst part of incarceration was not knowing how long they would remain prisoners. Eventually the war would end, but when? Each year, non-Jewish prisoners retained the hope that the war would be over by Christmas and they would be reunited with their families, but as each Christmas passed, this hope withered. "If I had known that I was to be in solitary for two years and then sent home it would have been certainly easier to bear than the constant and nagging uncertainty," [72] wrote Captain Vietor. He claimed this plagued him more than any other facet of prison camp.

Commander Donald Giles wrote that American POWs did not think they would be captives for as long as they were. Each year brought renewed hope that this would be the year of liberation, but as the year wound down, frus-

tration set in. The day when American troops charged into camp and freed everyone seemed distant and unreachable, and reunions with loved ones appeared even farther off.

Some could not cope well and experienced what prisoners called "going around

The face of this American POW shows the mental anguish he has endured in captivity. Coping with hardship was a matter of life and death in the camps.

the bend." They became inattentive and lay on their bunks, daydreaming of better times. One officer sat in a German prison hospital all day long, playing a violin. Without the violin, he was moody and subject to fits of anger.

Another prisoner of the Germans blamed himself for the loss of his bomber crew. Distraught over the deaths, he stared into space most of the time. One day he walked to the barbed wire fence and made a vain effort to scale it, which usually resulted in being shot by the guards, but the Germans realized the man was mentally unbalanced and simply removed him from the fence.

The men talked about all sorts of issues in their conversations, but the importance of certain items varied according to conditions in the camp. Sergeant Forrest Knox said that "as a gauge to judge a camp, if all we talked about was food, we were starving. If all we talked about was home, we were being treated rough and our minds dwelled on happier times. If all we talked about was women, we were well fed and had a soft detail."[73]

Food often dominated prisoners' thoughts. To get some form of meat into their diets, men in Japanese camps ate any creature that moved, from stray dogs to lizards and snakes. Captain Vietor claimed that the men at Stalag Luft I yearned for food first, then warmth, cigarettes, books, and human companionship. Relationships with women fared poorly in their list, because "when a man is constantly hungry it is difficult for him to think of anything but food."[74]

One of the favorite pastimes at Zentsuji was to reminisce about popular American restaurants. Men described entire meals they had enjoyed, shared favorite recipes, and listed in minute detail the first dinner they would eat upon returning home. According to Giles, all agreed upon one fact— "no one who is a prisoner of the Japanese will ever complain again about food. He has already experienced the worst."[75]

American prisoners of war in Germany were irritated with the news from home that German prisoners of war in the United States resided in warm barracks, ate decent food, and had plenty of recreation. Many German prisoners, while they missed their homeland and units, compared their stay in America to a vacation. Captain Vietor wrote that "the treatment of German prisoners in America was a sore point with us. Rumors that they were attending dances, given rations of beer, steak, ice cream, etc., made us seethe in envy."[76]

Honorable treatment of Germans by American authorities probably created better conditions for Americans in German hands, although this was small solace to them. POWs under Japanese control fared worse, as usual, because so few Japanese surrendered. American authorities had no large bloc of Japanese prisoners under their supervision.

In German camps, boredom was more of a problem than in the Pacific, especially for the officers. Men devised different hobbies to pass the time. One man laboriously counted every barb in the barbed wire in his compound, and one group of airmen argued for months about how a fly performed the feat of landing on the ceiling. An airman recalled the discussion

> went on all summer. A fly apparently flew with his feet below him but had to land with them above him. You couldn't answer the question by watching him do it. They flew around and around in circles, and when they decided to land they did it so suddenly there was no way to observe their method. We watched flies for months and never resolved anything.[77]

Americans grew tired of waiting for other things. Private George Davis said there were "lines for food, lines for the smelly latrines, lines for washing, lines for water, lines for cooking, lines for *Appell* (roll call), lines for everything of importance, it seemed."[78]

Men in Pacific camps detested having to bow to every Japanese soldier, no matter what rank. The Japanese ordered them to "stand erect; hold arms and hands straight down the sides; and bow from the waist, holding the back stiff, about thirty degrees from the erect position."[79]

The thing that most angered prisoners, however, was any hint of collaboration with the enemy. Collaboration included spying on fellow prisoners, to merely being friendly with certain guards. A man could be hostile, sullen, depressed, and a general nuisance to everyone, but he must never help the captors. Though collaboration rarely occurred, other prisoners shunned the offender. A handful of collaborators was even court-martialed after the war.

The Will to Survive

One of the most perplexing questions to ponder is what makes one man survive a horrendous situation when the man next to him, similar in most ways, dies. The issue has little connection to intelligence, size, or social standing, for men with similar characteristics met a variety of outcomes. Basically,

U.S. prisoners in the Pacific receive their daily ration of soup. POWs grew weary of standing in line for meals, roll call, washing, and latrines.

the men who came home coped because they formulated methods to deal with their situations. It did not always matter what the method was, as long as the man had a system upon which to rely.

Some turned to humor and laughter. One man said "there was more laughter in that dreary camp, even in the depths of winter, than back at our training camps in the U. S. where we had plenty of sunshine and more food than we could eat. We didn't laugh from gaiety, but because we wanted to retain our sanity."[80]

A marine who served on Wake Island joined three other men in camp and said

Hatred Helps You Survive

Some strong emotion needed to exist in each man if he was to endure. Some men hated the enemy, others loved their religion. In Donald Knox's book *Death March: The Survivors of Bataan*, Private Robert Brown tells how he survived his bitter days in a Japanese camp located in China:

What I did to survive, rather than pine for my parents—I knew it was a fictitious feeling and certainly not a lasting one—I made myself hate them. It was easier there to hate than to love. Whenever they came into my mind, I'd kick them out. "I'm mad at you. You're back in the States and you're not writing me." It was just one method to endure the anguish. When I got home I told my folks what I'd done, and they sat there with their eyes open; "I don't believe what you're saying." I said, "Don't take it that way. I had to. You were back here. You had access to food. I had to take care of myself. I couldn't have you in my heart and be pining over someone like that."

the Catholic rosary each night of his incarceration. When asked fifty years later what made him survive, he reached into his pocket, pulled out a worn rosary—the same one he had carried in camp—and said, "This. This is what got us through."[81]

Others relished smaller items which they may not have noticed back home. Private Eddy Laursen took time each day in the Philippines to stare at the sky. "The thing that really helped me was to lay down on the ground and to look up in the sky and try to shut out everything else. If I could look at something that wasn't contaminated by man, it would give me a real uplift. I especially liked the sunsets."[82]

Many men, surrounded by despicable conditions, used hatred to survive. The emotion seemed to spark an inner strength in most men and give them a reason to stay alive. One prisoner vowed to remain alive so that after liberation, he could kill the Japanese guard he had grown to hate. Forrest Knox explained that

if you hated, . . . it seems strange but those that did—I mean hated real hard—they lived. Those that started begging for their mothers, then you'd better start digging a hole for them. Once you felt sorry for yourself, you were an absolute gone bastard.[83]

Ironically, the younger captives often fared poorest. Veterans claimed that while they had faced other difficult times, the younger soldiers had never been so severely tested. Besides, most older men felt a powerful emotional connection to wives and children in the States, while many younger soldiers did not have wives or children.

William Nolan recalled one eighteen-year-old farm boy who was constantly homesick for his mother. Rather than cast aside such thoughts and face his situation, the youth told everyone that he could not live under such horrible conditions,

> and he just sat down and that was it—it was all too much for him. You couldn't do anything for him once he made up his mind. For instance, we'd eat anything to stay alive, but this young kid said of the rice that he couldn't eat this slop. Well, you either ate it or you died. He died.[84]

An inner toughness, then, appears to have been the most common quality of those who came home. For those who endured, they learned that they could face a crisis and emerge triumphant. They encountered the worst that anyone could imagine and came out in one piece. John Vietor wrote that "the daily uncertainty of never knowing if and when liberation would come gave many men the fortitude to han-

A cross and a bag containing cremated remains mark the final resting place of a dead prisoner of war. Little could be done to help those who lost the will to survive.

dle any situation, however difficult, that might crop up later in civilian life."[85]

They would need that fortitude, for as the war neared its end, conditions rapidly deteriorated for American prisoners in Europe and the Pacific.

Chapter 6

"We Are Free!"

A casual observer might think that as the war's end drew closer, morale in prison camps would have improved. In some cases, prisoners' spirits did rise, but for most prisoners the reverse was more common. As liberation approached, conditions deteriorated, dangers mounted, and frustrations multiplied.

"I Can Hear Them Coming"

"Under normal circumstances we might have been able to accept the worsening conditions philosophically," wrote Commander Donald Giles.

> We knew it was because our forces were hammering the Japanese, but we had been through so very much. We had been kicked, beaten, and harassed. We had seen friends beheaded and disemboweled. We were suffering the effects of severe malnutrition. Petty jealousies were beginning to surface among us, and arguments were

becoming commonplace. Morale was very low.[86]

No matter how miserable the men were, at least they now had visible evidence that American forces were winning the war. Listening to rumors about victories is one thing; seeing American aircraft drop bombs is another. Major E. R. Fendall scribbled in his Cabanatuan diary that September 21, 1944, was the happiest day of his life because for the first time the men spotted American fighters and bombers flying toward Manila.

Another prisoner stared in disbelief at first, then allowed happier thoughts to pour in. "We believed it. They could be none other but ours. And at that moment patriotism returned; love of country, love of our own magnificence, pride of being the biggest and best."[87]

At Stalag Luft I the men watched in awe as countless bombers flew overhead to attack Berlin. "You could hear them coming long before they came into sight. Then they

passed overhead in a gigantic, relentless mass. We would jump up and down, wave our arms, and yell our heads off."[88]

Besides viewing American aircraft, the prisoners in both German and Japanese camps noticed other signs indicating that the war fared poorly for their captors. Because heavy casualties necessitated that every available man be called for duty on the front lines, regular army guards were replaced by young boys or older men, and fewer new American prisoners entered

U.S. Navy aircraft bomb Manila in September 1944. The sight of American planes attacking Japanese targets brought renewed hope and patriotism to U.S. POWs in the Pacific.

camp. Work details that left German prison camps saw lines of wounded enemy soldiers and homeless citizens congesting the roads, while men in the Pacific observed that the Japanese civilians looked dejected.

The devastation suffered by the Germans was all too apparent. Louis Grivetti's work crew had to remove dead bodies from the town of Dresden, which was hideously destroyed in fire bombings in February 1945.

> We knew at the time that many people had been killed, but we didn't know there were tens of thousands. The dead were just piled up in the bomb shelters where they had been asphyxiated [suffocated]. We had to wear rags around our faces because of the fumes and the stench. We would simply tie a rope around their ankles and drag them out to this open area

where we stacked them, and the Germans eventually burned them.[89]

Plans for Removal

As the American military moved relentlessly forward, both German and Japanese authorities intended to move the prisoners farther from the fighting. Japan planned to use the men as bargaining chips with the American government, but Japan's military leaders did not want to be humiliated by losing

Dresden lies in charred ruins after being firebombed. Scenes such as this gave prisoners an idea of how poorly the war was going for their captors.

prisoners to American forces, especially since those men could testify to the harsh treatment they had received.

American captives, fearing mass slaughter as the war wound down, organized steps to prevent it. Men fashioned weapons out of wood or eating utensils in case executions started. Some camps planned a general attack on enemy guards, even though they realized many would die in the attempt. Not much could be done, but the men intended to at least make it more difficult for their captors to enact large-scale killings.

President Harry S Truman, who had succeeded Franklin D. Roosevelt after his death in 1945, feared for the safety of American prisoners. He announced that he was determined to do everything possible to help them and to bring about their release as soon as possible. Consequently, on July 26, 1945, the United States, Great Britain, and the Soviet Union stated that stern justice would be handed out to all war criminals, including those who had mistreated prisoners.

Less Food, More Death

Ironically, as American bombers in Europe and submarines in the Pacific tightened the noose on the enemy, they also made life more miserable for prisoners. The simple

The leaders of Great Britain, the United States, and the Soviet Union—Winston Churchill, Harry S Truman, and Joseph Stalin—meet in July 1945. They declared that those who mistreated POWs would be severely punished.

fact that hungry, weakened men had to endure a journey to another location proved more than some could bear. Red Cross parcels and other supplies could no longer get through. Hungry men even battled with rodents for the meager amounts of food remaining. Commander Donald Giles reported that "the rats were becoming bolder, vying with us for what little food we had. They were starving also."[90]

Prisoners' lives were also endangered from high-flying American bombers. In December 1944, ninety-one American aircraft destroyed the Manchurian Aircraft Manufacturing Company in China. Unfortunately, the pilots were unaware that some bombs fell directly into a prison camp and killed nineteen American prisoners. The following

"He Dropped Like a Sack of Potatoes"

American paratrooper George Rosie was captured on June 6, 1944—D Day—and incarcerated at Stalag IIIB. In January 1945, with the Russian Army drawing closer, the Germans moved Rosie and the others farther away. Rosie describes his forced march in Lewis H. Carlson's *We Were Each Other's Prisoners*:

The Germans gave us some old overcoats which were indeed a blessing, but no one had hats, gloves, or boots. And it was cold! I mean to tell you it was down around zero. The guards kept us moving all afternoon and all night, with three short breaks. We were carrying everything we could, but it was getting so tough people just started pitching things. We stopped by some barns about five o'clock the next afternoon. One POW walked over to an old German woman standing by her fence and tried to trade a bar of soap for some food. One of the guards walked up behind him and smacked him in the back of the head with his rifle butt. He dropped like a sack of potatoes. As we were marched into the barn, we walked by him but there was no sign of life. The back of his head was smashed in and he was bleeding profusely.

May, sixty-two American captives perished in the ferocious Tokyo fire bombings.

Death came from the enemy as well. After American bombers hit a Japanese airfield on the island of Palawan, the commander of a nearby prison camp ordered the Americans executed. Japanese guards surrounded the camp on three sides—an imposing cliff formed the fourth—poured gasoline into the entrances where 150 American captives lived, and set the buildings on fire. As Americans rushed out of the flames, the guards either gunned them down or bayoneted them. Here and there a man made it safely to the camp's fence facing the cliff, squeezed underneath the wire, and dropped from ledge to ledge to the beach below. Though Japanese soldiers shot most who fled this way, eleven men survived the Palawan massacre.

Up One Day, Down the Next

Corresponding to the events which swirled about them, prisoners' emotions fluctuated from day to day. Ecstasy over possible liberation mingled with fear of death or that the war would continue for months. The jubilant news that on June 6, 1944, American and British troops finally landed on Europe's beaches at Normandy boosted every prisoner's morale, just as did news that General Douglas MacArthur had successfully commanded an enormous American force to recapture the Philippine Islands. News of a July 1944 attempt to kill Hitler lifted spirits, and some prisoners began to believe they might be home for Christmas.

When war's fortunes turned sour for the Americans in December 1944 with the German advance in the Battle of the Bulge, prisoners again faced the prospect of languishing in camp. When large groups of freshly captured American soldiers were marched into camp by German guards, morale plummeted to an all-time low.

Some prisoners worried they would not live to see liberation. One captive in the Pacific wrote,

> It all seems to me that an appreciable [large] number of POWs do not feel secure at all. We do expect the end of the war, but we worry that it will also mean an end for us personally. I can-

U.S. soldiers taken prisoner during the Battle of the Bulge are marched to camp. The sight of freshly captured troops was a blow to the morale of American POWs in Germany.

not help being reminded of a tunnel that progressively seals off the closer one comes to its end.[91]

Death Marches and Other Atrocities

Most disturbing to the men was the possibility of forced marches to spots farther from friendly forces. In weakened condition, many feared that they could not survive a trek across German lands or a journey inside the hold of a freighter fleeing the Philippines for Japan.

In April 1945 Robert Engstrom and other Americans walked one hundred miles from Nuremberg to Stalag VIIA. Though most survived the fifteen-day trek, a few did not. Two men attempted to run into nearby forests, but German soldiers unleashed guard dogs which tore the men to pieces. A Texan named Kenneth Simmons battled frigid temperatures and lack of nourishment on his January 1945 march out of camp, but lived to tell of the ordeal. "I must have said it a thousand times. I am one step nearer home, and I am going to take another."[92]

Angry Japanese guards moved Donald Giles and the other men at Zentsuji to another camp set in isolated mountains. The Americans doubted their survival. One prisoner said, "It was logical to believe that machine-gunning in a mountain retreat was the most sensible means of extermination. . . . The next three months [before liberation] did little to lift our spirits, except that each morning found us alive. These months were a nightmare of brutality, mass punishments, and constant beatings."[93]

Little that occurred during the war's final months match the infamous "Hell Ships" in barbarity. Seeking to transport American captives speedily out of the Philippines, the Japanese crammed hundreds of sick men into the stifling holds of ships, closed all but a few hatches, and headed to sea with little food or water. As the days passed in the tropical sun, starved and thirsty men wailed for nourishment. Some went insane in the 125-degree heat and cut themselves to drink their own blood.

Justice Meted Out

Americans detested any prisoner who willingly worked with the enemy. They had their own methods of handling these individuals. In a few cases, retaliation could be severe, as Robert Engstrom relates in Lewis H. Carlson's *We Were Each Other's Prisoners*. He and other Americans started on a long march from one camp to another, and the journey provided them a chance to exact punishment:

> Many of us were pretty weak, and we would try to help each other. But there was one fellow we didn't help. He had been collaborating with the Germans. We knew about it in part because he had gained weight while the rest of us were losing. He'd disappear in the evening and then somehow get back to the barracks. Everybody hated his guts, but we just left him alone. No one talked to him or had anything to do with him. The guards told us during the march that if anyone couldn't make it, he would be disposed of. . . . So this fat guy was walking along, and it wasn't too long until he was huffing and puffing and telling us he couldn't walk anymore. We told him we couldn't help him. So he fell off to the side of the road, and we heard a shot. That's all there was to it.

In one ship the Japanese guards became so angry at the yelling from below that they threatened to cover the few open hatches and cut off all supply of air. A new rule thus quickly entered, recalled prisoner Forrest Knox. "The crazy ones, they howled because they were afraid to die—but now the ground rules changed. If they howled, they died. The screaming stopped. . . . In the hold of that ship you executed those that were an absolute danger to you."[94]

Another man wanted water so badly he tried to scratch through the ship's metal hold to get at the water outside. "For hours he scratched and scratched," Knox wrote. "This noise infuriated me immensely. No matter how I tried to isolate my mind from it, the noise cut through me." When Knox asked him what he was doing, the man replied he was making a hole. "There's water out there. I can hear it."[95]

Captain Marion Lawton saw actions he thought impossible, until the Hell Ships:

They went mad [from thirst]. Some drank urine. Some turned vampire. They tried to drink the blood of the sick men who couldn't resist. Men were murdered on that ship. . . . I was next to an old college classmate of mine. His arms were badly scratched. I asked him what had happened. He told me it was nothing. "It's more than nothing," I said. "Who did this to you?" "Well, I fought off a feller for half the night who was trying to cut me so he could drink my blood. He was mad."[96]

Those who survived the forced marches or Hell Ships now had to control their emotions and wait for liberation by American forces. Since no one knew when that might be, each day turned into one long ordeal.

Liberation in Germany

Freedom, the moment all prisoners had anticipated since their first day of incarceration, came surprisingly quickly and quietly for many in Europe. On April 30, 1945, at Stalag Luft I, one prisoner walked out of his barracks to fetch some water but came hurriedly back proclaiming the guards had disappeared. With the approach of the Russian army, the Germans fled to avoid being taken captive, leaving the camp in the hands of the prisoners. When the Russians arrived shortly after, they brought cows, pigs, and sheep into Stalag Luft I so the men could enjoy a feast.

U.S. infantrymen use their weapons to open the gate of a German prison camp. Liberation usually came quickly and quietly to POWs in Europe.

In another camp, Private Johnnie C. Womble realized something strange was occurring when the guards gathered the prisoners into two barns near camp and explained that they were shielding them from marauding groups of troops, who wanted to slaughter all prisoners. The guards added that they planned to surrender to American forces, and they reassured Womble and the rest that they would tell the Americans where they could find the prisoners. A few days later an American patrol arrived to take Womble's group to safety.

Private George Davis received a hint of his freedom from a guard he had befriended. One day the German informed him General George Patton (an American military commander) was in southern Germany and the war would soon be over. On his day of liberation Davis exchanged addresses with the guard, and the two continued to correspond and visit each other until the German's death in the early 1980s.

While men's emotions upon liberation varied from ecstasy to silent satisfaction, most erupted in complete joy. At long last their struggle to remain alive seemed over. Home beckoned; families appeared closer; good food, decent clothes, and the simple joys of living in the United States flooded their minds. When Patton's Third Army liberated one camp in Bavaria a prisoner yelled, "It's over! The battle is over! We are free!" [97]

The ex-prisoners enjoyed their first moments of freedom in different ways. Some took revenge upon the Germans. Robert

Engstrom stated that one of the most hated chores in camp was being forced to pull what was called the "honey wagon," a cart in which excrement was collected.

> But now we thought it might be kind of fun to have the guards drag it around. We all cheered while they pushed and pulled it. The Russians [prisoners at the camp] then decided they would also have some fun. They lined up about ten of the guards just like we did, but they took the first guy

After hearing that freedom is at hand, these POWs joyfully display an American flag they have kept hidden in their camp.

and just slit his throat from ear to ear. They did the same thing to each of those Germans.[98]

American medical teams entered camps to start the lengthy process of examining the men and preparing them for the trip home. Mess kitchens quickly delivered plates of hot food and milk, and men received stationery so they could write loved ones. Eventually, the freed prisoners were given passes to head into nearby German towns, where they were surprised at the calm reaction of citizens toward their victorious enemy.

The Atom Bomb

While no single event caused the Germans to surrender in May 1945, the same cannot be stated for Japan. Facing the possibility of invading the Japanese home islands and suffering large numbers of casualties, American military strategists and politicians decided to employ the most powerful weapon then devised—the atom bomb. American president Harry S Truman hoped to shock the Japanese into surrender.

On August 6, 1945, an atom bomb killed more than one-hundred thousand people in Hiroshima, Japan, including twenty-three American captives in Hiroshima Castle. Within a few days American prisoners throughout Japan learned that something had happened. On August 8 one prisoner wrote in his diary, "Today, we heard

The atom bombs that destroyed the cities of Hiroshima and Nagasaki (pictured) also brought a quick end to the war in the Pacific.

the most sensational rumor of our camp life: The Americans dropped a large bomb on Japan that killed hundreds of thousands of people. No one, of course, really believes this—it seems so unlikely—that one bomb could do so much damage."[99]

At some camps prisoners suddenly received harsher treatment. When POW officers inquired why, they were told it was because the United States had used an inhumane weapon.

Two days after Hiroshima, a second atom bomb destroyed the Japanese city of

Nagasaki and thirty thousand more people. American POW Melvin Routt was working at his farm detail thirty miles from Nagasaki when he saw a mushroom cloud rise in the distant sky, followed by the sound of a terrific explosion and a ferocious wind. In another camp Lieutenant Julien Goodman heard a tremendous roar. The building in which he stood then shook so hard he thought it would collapse.

The destructive power of the atom bombs had its desired effect. On August 15, Emperor Hirohito of Japan announced his nation's surrender. At the same time the War Ministry ordered prison camp officers to destroy anything that might incriminate Japan in prison atrocities, and it sent a notice that "personnel who mistreated prisoners of war and internees or who are held in extremely bad sentiment by them are permitted to take care of it by immediately transferring or by fleeing without a trace." [100]

Suddenly, in many camps the Japanese guards changed their behavior. On August 10, Rabbi Nussbaum, a chaplain in one of the camps, recorded that the Japanese were much kinder to them and that everyone knew the war's end was near. The Japanese even permitted the prisoners to listen to a shortwave radio. A few days later the commandant of another camp announced that the Americans would no longer have to work, and guards no longer prowled the grounds. Cigarettes, fruit, and other items suddenly became available, and the prisoners could freely move about. The reason for these mysterious changes was clarified when the Japanese commandant informed senior American officers that the war had ended.

While much debate exists as to the moral correctness of using an atom bomb, it may have saved many prisoners' lives. The unbelievable destructiveness handed the Japanese an excuse for ending the war. Without this, they may have continued to fight, believing that to give in would be a sign of cowardice and a national humiliation.

Liberation in Japan

In Sian in Manchuria, General Jonathan Wainwright was playing his 8,632nd game of solitaire when he learned that the war was over. At Cabanatuan in the Philippines, the commandant told the American officers, "You are now free Americans. You are no longer the responsibility of the Japanese Empire. We will leave you rations for thirty days and you will be safe if you stay within the barbed wire." [101] He and the guards then fled to avoid capture by American forces.

At Nakhon Nayok in Thailand, the British, American, and Australian prisoners stood silent for a moment after hearing from senior officers of the war's end. Suddenly, the twenty thousand weary men erupted in cheers, hugging, and backslapping. The three nationalities then sang their respective national anthems, with the Americans substituting "God Bless America" because it more closely mirrored their emotions.

"Cheers from freedom-starved throats drown out the rest of the speaker's voice,"

The Grand Old Flag

Few sights could have been more emotional to American prisoners than watching the American flag rise to the top of a flagpole. After lengthy years of torment, to see the symbol of their nation once again proudly snap in the breeze was more than many could take. In the book *Captive of the Rising Sun*, marine Major Donald Spicer explains one special moment when the men unfurled a flag which had been secretly hidden since their imprisonment four years earlier. Spicer was selected to raise the flag, since he had been the man forced to take down the colors when captured on Guam.

> And there, 45 months after I tasted the bitter dregs of humiliation—almost 4 years after I became the first U. S. Marine to strike our colors to an enemy—I was to raise the first American flag over the Japanese homeland.

My feelings, therefore, as I reverently held the flag in my hands and proudly marched up the hill to the flagpole on September 2, 1945, are not difficult to imagine. With a final caress, I let that Grand Old Flag slip through my fingers, to flutter proudly over the Japanese homeland. As I gazed upward and saluted the Stars and Stripes, I swallowed hard, restraining my tears. After we were dismissed, I let them flow freely, laughing and crying at the same time as we milled about wringing each other's hands.

> Every man . . . was filled with the same surging emotions. Every man was holding on with his last ounce of strength, determined to prove that he came from fighting stock which could not be beaten.

recorded one prisoner upon receiving the welcome news. "Men hug men. Some are crying, proudly allowing the tears to flow down their thin faces, over prominent cheek bones, and drip on thin chests."[102]

Ironically, though they were now free men, many Americans could not leave their camps because dense jungle surrounded them. Even if they had access to vehicles, a large number were too weak to endure any lengthy trip. They had little choice but to wait for American soldiers to arrive.

In the home islands of Japan, American ex-POWs boarded trains and traveled about. They walked into restaurants and appeared in public places without any animosity shown by the defeated civilians. One group of Americans entering Yokohama on a train spotted a group of Japanese who had been injured in an earlier train accident. They quickly gathered whatever supplies they had, such as canned food and a few blankets, and offered the items to the injured.

While some Americans had anticipated the moment for years when they would be able to get revenge on despised prison guards, few instances of reprisal occurred. The men still lived amidst an ocean of Japanese, and until American troops joined them, it was better to rest or tour the countryside and calmly wait for their countrymen to take control.

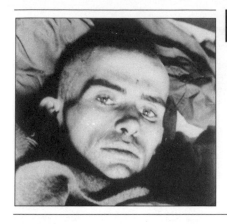

Chapter 7

"I Will Never Be Free of Those Prison Years"

S ince their time in captivity was over, American prisoners, now called ex-POWs, entered the lengthy process of rehabilitation and readjustment to life back in the United States. For many, this would prove a difficult task, as problems beset them at each stage. The former prisoners of war were about to start on their next battle—the war for normalcy.

Processing the Men

In Europe, American medical teams moved in to evaluate and process the prisoners. Physicians checked each man for illnesses and weaknesses, and clerks handed over a sheath of forms for the men to fill out. Once the initial processing ended, the men were transported to an enormous tent city in France called Camp Lucky Strike, where they passed through final evaluations before being shipped home.

A fleet of American aircraft evacuated the men at Stalag Luft I in one day. Army private Philip Miller recalled, "We marched

out in a long column. The P.A. system was blasting 'You Gotta Accentuate the Positive.' The B-17s [bombers] came in one minute apart. Fifty men were loaded in about twenty seconds and took off."[103]

A day of boundless joy turned tragic for one group of fifty ex-POWs. Corporal Robert Engstrom stepped onto his transport for shipment to Camp Lucky Strike and watched the aircraft immediately ahead take off. The plane started down the runway, which was slippery from a steady drizzle, but could not gain sufficient power to lift off the ground. The pilot tried to stop his aircraft, but it slid off the runway to the left and burst into flames. Engstrom saw four men jump out of the transport, but the others were trapped in the inferno and died. The incident was a stark reminder that while the war may have been officially over, danger remained.

Though the United States and the Soviet Union agreed that any soldiers they liberated would be quickly handed over, most

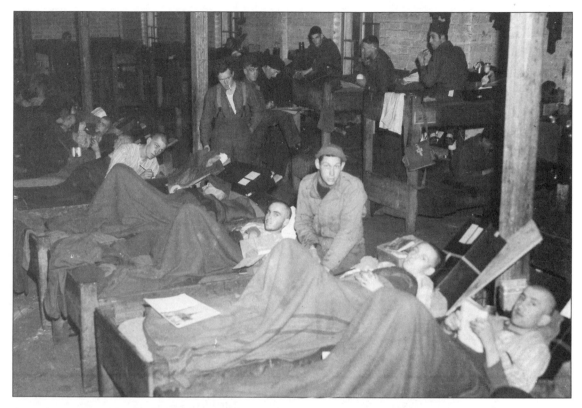

Weakened by months or even years of malnutrition, these ex-POWs await medical care during processing in Germany.

Americans freed by the Russian army had to wait to rejoin their units. Though they were not mistreated, the process took a month or more longer than for those liberated by American forces.

At Camp Lucky Strike, the men again went through a series of medical exams and filled out more questionnaires. They had plenty of food available, but doctors warned the men to go easy until their stomachs had an opportunity to adjust to the richer diet. In the meantime, they were to rebuild their strength slowly. One day a group of beautiful women visited the camp to entertain the men. A Red Cross worker noticed that few men attended the show. When she asked a man why, he replied, "Well, ma'am, they are feeding me 12 vitamin pills a day now, but before I'll be interested in women again they'll have to feed me 24." [104]

Different problems existed in the Pacific, where almost two hundred prison camps were spread out across Asia and the islands. Thus, more time was required to reach and assist the former prisoners. General Douglas MacArthur, commander of American forces in the Pacific, organized

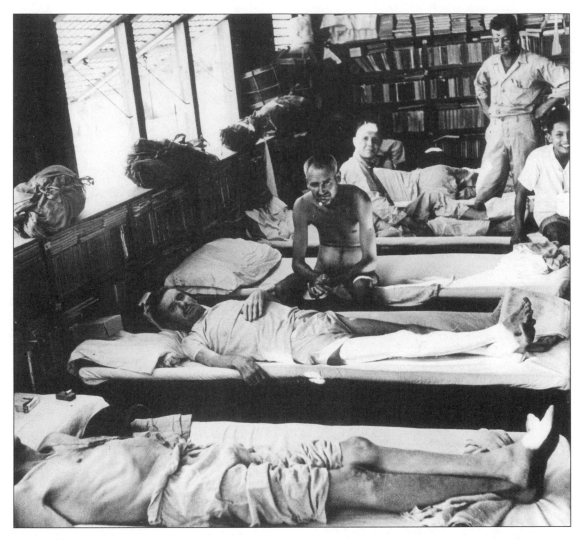

In the Philippines, inmates of a Japanese camp anticipate the arrival of help. The distances between camps in the Pacific made rescue efforts more difficult.

twenty-eight teams each containing one officer and three enlisted men, and handed them the task of locating and returning all POWs in the Pacific.

American aircraft dropped thousands of leaflets announcing the war's end and telling prisoners to remain in camp until assistance arrived. Soon other aircraft parachuted in much-needed food, medical supplies, and relief teams. In a few cases, American parachute teams arrived in prison camps before the Japanese commandant even knew that the war had ended.

The food reached welcome hands. Commander Donald Giles related that

we witnessed the most beautiful sight any of us had ever seen. Out came a flock of brightly colored cargo-carrying parachutes. . . . Suddenly the sky was filled with spots of red, green, blue, yellow, and white as the parachutes and their cargo drifted down to the ground in the vicinity of our camp.[105]

Delighted men tore open the containers to find an amazing array of candy, milk, and other foods. Though doctors in the camps warned men about overeating, just as doctors had done in Europe, many men devoured everything they touched.

In one case, the parachuted food proved lethal. Navy aircraft made a final food drop to one camp on September 9, 1945. Three Americans were killed when one of the huge food drums burst upon hitting the ground and propelled its contents at the unfortunate men.

On September 3, 1945, the hospital ship *Marigold* docked at Yokohama and sent teams across Japan. Soldiers and medical teams that arrived at the Japanese camps were shocked at what they found. After hasty examinations, doctors recorded that at least 60 percent of the men suffered from internal parasites, 50 percent from anemia, and 77 percent from beriberi. Many prisoners lost their eyesight or endured painful swellings of legs and arms because of vitamin deficiency. The prisoners at one camp were so undernourished that when the relief team handed out coffee, they became ill from the caffeine.

"How different they looked from those we had seen prior to our capture!" wrote Commander Giles when the first American military personnel arrived. He added that "from the looks on their faces and their expressions of disbelief, we knew that this must have been a first for them also."[106]

By the end of September, most ex-POWs had been removed from their camps and shipped to the Twenty-ninth Replacement Depot south of Manila, in the Philippines. There they received new uniforms, additional medical care, mail from home, and back pay.

One task awaited the men before heading home—they had to fill out lengthy questionnaires about their prison experiences. The information was mainly intended to be used as evidence in future war crimes trials against Japanese officers and guards, but the men approached the job with hesitation. "Strangely, these last questions were difficult to answer," claimed Giles. "We had buried some experiences, repressed some memories. These were some things we wanted above all to forget."[107] Those memories the men tried to forget would return to haunt them in the form of flashbacks and nightmares for years to come.

Home Sweet Home

Most American prisoners of war started their trip home within six weeks after liberation. Though the men in the Pacific reached the United States after those in Europe because the war against Japan ended three months later, their homecoming experiences were similar.

Corporal Kenneth Day embarked upon a three-day train trip across Japan to reach his American transport, and along the way his jubilation turned to quiet reflection:

> On the first day we saw towns that had been leveled by fire. We cheered. We could look all the way from one edge of a town to the other and not see one thing standing. . . . By the time we had passed a dozen such cities and towns, we stopped cheering. The devastation was so total that it overpowered our senses. . . . By the second day we said little, but just stared out the windows.

I had come to loathe and despise these people, but this was almost too much.[108]

Commander Giles had another worry. When he arrived at the USS *Indiana* for shipment home, he feared that his ragged appearance would so shock fellow American naval officers that they would not let him board. "Were I that officer [the officer of the deck], I asked myself, would I allow anyone who looked so disreputable to come aboard?" After being assisted up the ladder by a young seaman in an immaculate white

Little is left of a Japanese city after an American air raid. The sight of so much destruction was sobering to ex-prisoners of war.

uniform, Giles was warmly greeted by both the officer of the deck and the ship's captain, who were saluting. "Although not yet home in Annapolis [Maryland], I knew that I was among my own."[109]

The men relaxed, caught up on sleep, ate food, and chatted with friends as the ships inched their way across the oceans to the United States. When Giles reached Honolulu, Hawaii, the city paid for each man to telephone home. As Giles had not spoken with his wife in three and a half years, he wondered how it would go. "How would she sound? What would I say? It did not take long for the connection to be made, and suddenly the years fell away."[110]

Incredible sights and emotions unfurled as the ships from Europe or Japan entered New York, Boston, or San Francisco. Captain John Vietor wrote of landing at Boston that "there was a brass band, Red Cross girls with coffee to meet us and a few casual onlookers. We weren't worried about what kind of reception we had. We were home at last."[111]

A similar experience hit Private Lawrence E. Roberts as he returned from Stalag VIIB on June 5, 1945. "I can remember pulling into New York and passing the Statue of Liberty. All of us were quiet as we passed by her. Some men were crying, others were praying, I was doing both. It was the happiest day of my life. I will never forget that day—never."[112]

Commander Giles, who so eloquently recorded his thoughts in his memoir, summarized the emotions in a few simple words

A Warm Welcome

Most returning ex-prisoners landed to joyous receptions in the United States. Cities organized parades, businesses welcomed the men, and town governments issued proclamations of praise. In his book *Captive of the Rising Sun*, Commander Donald T. Giles quotes from a program issued by San Francisco, California, upon his return.

The Golden Gate . . . is symbolic of San Francisco's open arms of welcome and the people of this city are proud it is here that you first set foot on your own land and breathe the pure air of God's country.

We feel that our reception to you is indicative of the national feeling towards all liberated prisoners of war.

The privilege is ours of rejoicing with your loved ones on your liberation and safe return. The privations and suffering which you have so heroically endured, the humiliations to which you have been subjected, are over. While we hope the thought of them will be speedily erased from your memories, these sacrifices of yours will not be forgotten by us.

The city that "sitteth at the Western Gate" bids you a hearty welcome home.

as his ship neared California. "The good old United States looked so beautiful that morning. It was grand to be home."[113]

Early Fears

Many ex-POWs worried that either they had so changed, or that their nation, occupations, and families had been so altered, that they could not successfully readjust to civilian life. In the peacefulness at home, could the former prisoner rapidly shift gears and drop the defenses accumulated during captivity?

One of the first tasks they faced was unpleasant for the former prisoners. The United States government again asked every ex-POW to give more statements about the treatment they received from their former captors. To prosecute German and Japanese leaders in the war crimes trials then occurring, government lawyers required evidence. The former prisoners were seen as excellent providers of the missing information.

However, most wanted to avoid reliving painful experiences. Many gave sworn statements and thus avoided having to travel back to Japan or Germany, but the ordeal left them feeling uncomfortable nonetheless. They were eager to forget the past and resume their lives.

Their discomfort did not diminish with the results of the war crimes trials. Though a handful of Japanese and German leaders were executed for their roles in the war, most received prison sentences ranging up to twenty-five years, and few served more than ten years. By 1958 all Japanese officials

Guards of a German prison camp are put on trial for war crimes. Ex-POWs were asked to give testimony against their former captors.

had been released, meaning that the men guilty for the incarceration and mistreatment of thousands of Americans spent a maximum of thirteen years in jail.

Guilt Leads to Repressed Memories

When the men rejoined friends and loved ones, they experienced feelings that soldiers who had not been captured did not have. Though society recognized survivors of Japanese and German prison camps as heroes, the men themselves often did not. Ex-prisoners of war felt shame that they had surrendered to the enemy, even if it had been unavoidable, and they felt guilty that they had survived when other prisoners had succumbed.

"For a long time I just tried to forget my experiences as a POW," claimed William Kalway, who was captured by the Germans at the Battle of Kasserine Pass on February 19, 1943. "In spite of trying to rationalize my capture by telling myself I had absolutely no other choice, deep inside I considered myself a coward."[114]

Commander Giles stated that he carried those feelings for years afterward. He said that he and others felt "that they had failed their country, their flag, and the traditions of the naval service; that they had failed the natives who had been entrusted to their care; that they had failed in their careers."[115]

After being captured in December 1944 and spending six months in a German prison camp, Louis G. Grivetti longed for one thing:

When I came back to the States I just tried to forget everything about being a POW. It's only been the last few years that I can recollect many of the things that went on. I have written a brief memoir, and little things keep coming back. But for years, like a lot of other guys, I just tried to wipe out my memory of the war and my imprisonment in Dresden.[116]

A former prisoner of the Japanese, Jack Brady, kept his emotions tightly bottled inside. "I couldn't talk to people. I couldn't even talk to my parents. They had an entirely different outlook on things. I had to move out. I couldn't talk to any of my old friends. They were entirely different. I shouldn't say they were, I was."[117]

Even popular books and movies about prison camps, such as *Stalag 17* and *The Great Escape*, tossed an additional burden at the men. They cast the American captives as fun-loving, brash soldiers who constantly harassed the enemy and continually tried to escape. While some truth existed in this depiction, it was far from realistic. Most men had simply tried to remain alive and outlast the war. Now, when people at home asked what camp was like, they expected an answer similar to what they read in books or saw at the movies.

Louis Grivetti created a simple solution. "You didn't tell anybody that you had been a POW. If you did, they would always ask, 'Why did you let them capture you? Why didn't you fight?' I put twenty-one years in

Movies such as The Great Escape *(pictured) gave the American public a misguided impression of what life in a prisoner-of-war camp was like.*

the army, but not a handful of people ever knew I was a POW."[118]

Nightmares and Lost Chances

Though they had been removed far from their prison camps, problems persisted for ex-POWs. Robert Engstrom seethed in anger in his first few days home at seeing German prisoners of war working as waiters at Fort Kilmore, New Jersey.

Well, we hit that first chow line, and there were all these big, husky, healthy-looking Germans. I tell you, it was a shock. There we were, a bunch of emaciated runts, nothing but skin and bones. . . . They obviously had enjoyed more than enough to eat, and we had not. They had been well treated, and we had suffered.[119]

Something as simple as possession of food, once taken for granted, now carried an importance it normally would not. Sandy Lubinski guarded against being without food by carrying bread in his pockets for almost two years after returning from Germany. Danny Abeles constantly made sure that a supply of food was at hand. "After I got home, I was always opening the refrigerator door. My mom would say, 'Go ahead and eat something.' I'd tell her, 'No, it's just nice to know there's food there.' I still cannot stand to waste any food."[120]

Commander Giles faced the stark realization that his beloved navy had passed him by. A new array of strategy and technology had altered the navy he knew in 1941, and younger officers had been promoted above him. At times he felt hopelessly behind.

When Giles sought refuge among family and friends, he encountered other problems.

> After so many years of confinement, I found the sudden reentry into civilization to be confusing. . . . It was wonderful to be back home with my family, friends, and neighbors, but the whirl of activity really bothered me. The pace of everyday life was so much faster than when I had left the United States four years earlier. So many changes had occurred during those years that I found it difficult to relate.[121]

Because of vitamin deficiency, Giles lost all his teeth within fifteen years. Because he suffered from nervousness and felt uncomfortable around others, he avoided large crowds for years.

Other men had spent two or three years in prison camp dreaming of returning to their loved ones, only to find drastically dif-

ferent conditions. The wife of one former prisoner sued for divorce even before he arrived back home. "The first time I saw my four-year-old son was in a lawyer's office in November of 1945."[122]

J. J. Carter had asked a girl to marry him before he left for service in 1941. When he arrived home, he "had the idea that everything stood still while I was gone. Nobody got older and nobody changed. On my first day home I chatted with my folks for a while, then, 'I guess I better run down and see Mavis.'"[123] His mom informed him that his fiancée had married someone else while Carter was in prison camp.

"Nobody Was on the Dock Waiting"

Since ex-POWs arrived in the United States at different times between May and October, the greetings received were not identical. As J. J. Carter explains in Donald Knox's *Death March: Survivors of Bataan*, some could be quite demoralizing to the returning soldiers.

> When we pulled alongside the dock [at San Francisco], there was just a sprinkling of people waiting for us. Come to find out, some of the people waiting were ex-wives who had remarried, thinking their husbands were dead. They'd come to San Francisco to get the thing straightened out.

> When I got off the boat, no folks were there to meet me, no friends, nobody. We lined up, were checked off, boarded a bus, and were carried to Letterman [General Hospital].

> I could never figure out why nobody was on that dock waiting for us. Everyone gathered on the rail and looked for someone.

Most showed symptoms of what is now called post-traumatic stress disorder. Frequent nightmares, flashbacks to prison camp, depression, and anger plagued some for years. Government studies indicated that while 25 percent of all veterans suffered from it, almost 90 percent of ex-POWs battled the malady.

Staff Sergeant Harold Feiner's nightmares disturbed the entire family, but he could do little to stop them except hope that time would ease the situation. "I know I climbed the wall and was drenched, when my wife would shake the hell out of me to wake me up. The children would come running into the room because they could hear me screaming." [124]

Half of the respondents to a government survey replied that they thought their lives would be shortened by at least ten years as a result of their confinements. One wrote on the form that he would be surprised if he lived beyond age fifty.

Daryle Watters resorted to a familiar method with which to cope with problems—he called upon his prison camp experiences. "When things got too difficult, I would get out the deck of cards and began [sic] playing solitaire just like I did when I was a prisoner." [125]

"Then You Fight Your Government"

While diverse government programs exist today for service personnel, none existed in 1945. Former prisoners of war were questioned, given food and clothing, possibly a welcome parade, then sent on their way. Instead of pouring out their burdens to psy-

The gaunt faces of three ex-POWs show the strain of incarceration. Post-traumatic stress disorder and shortened lives would haunt many who survived the camps.

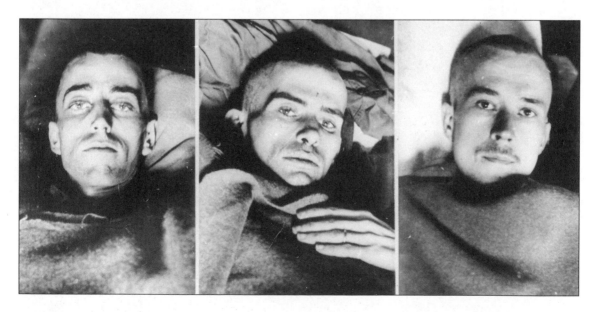

chiatrists, World War II prisoners who returned home had to handle the situation on their own and with the support of loved ones.

Physicians at veterans' hospitals rarely gave time to former prisoners. At most, they halfheartedly listened, then prescribed medication. One man recalled, "Nobody helped us with our transition to civilian life. The U.S. Army retrained its guard dogs but there were no programs for us POWs. I guess your family was supposed to be your psychiatrist."[126]

Rather than offer support, the government took a hard stance. Most ex-POWs, especially those from Japanese camps, suffered from heart and liver problems, diminished eyesight, and nervous disorders, but the Veterans Administration (VA) would not pay for treatment unless the men could prove their ailments were service-related. Since no records existed from prison camp, the men had nowhere to turn.

"When we got back, we weren't given any real counseling of any type," explained Robert Brown. "A lot of guys needed psychiatric help." He stated that when he walked into a VA hospital, "They tell us that we have to prove that our ailments are service-connected. Why should we have to prove it? The records are missing, if there ever were any. Think the Japs kept records of the beatings given us in Cabanatuan?"[127]

Consequently, a shocking number of men grew hostile to the government which apparently had abandoned them. "You fight a war, and then you fight your government

"No One Wanted Me"

Sergeant Forrest Knox saw sights in the Pacific which he can never forget, but following the war his anger was directed more against his government and American society. He recounted his story for Donald Knox in the book *Death March: The Survivors of Bataan*.

"No one helped [when I returned]. I felt utterly trapped. It was the toughest battle I fought and I fought it alone."

When Knox asked a former classmate for a job with General Motors, the friend declined. "You're a wreck. There is no way you could do a day's work, and we can't support you just because you're a veteran."

A frustrated Knox later exploded. "I was home, wasn't I? For four years I had clawed and fought and killed just to get back home. Now, no one wanted me or gave a shit if I had a place to live or a job to support a family."

harder than the war to get what you've got coming,"[128] John J. Foster stated.

Gradually, some assistance trickled in. By 1949 the government agreed to pay ex-POWs two dollars for each day they were in prison camps. After the Vietnam War, when many POWs wrote accounts and spoke out about their suffering, the military's views softened. In 1985 Congress created the Prisoner of War Medal to honor that forgotten group.

World War II ex-POWs gradually turned to each other for help. Most joined organizations such as the American Ex-Prisoners of War or the American Defenders of Bataan and Corregidor, where they found a sympathetic ear from others who had endured similar situations. As they confided in one another, the emotional scars began to heal.

A Mixed Legacy

Long after the war's end, ex-POWs continue to be affected by their experiences. Not only were those years lost as far as family and careers, but they retarded development in subsequent times.

One former prisoner "can't leave food on a plate. I even have problems leaving any gravy. I have to get a piece of bread and sop it up. My wife says I learned that I could take more than I thought I could. I did gain a lot of confidence, but that was because I had to."[129]

Part of the reason Robert Haney wrote a book about his experience as a POW was so his children could understand him. "Perhaps they will gain insight into why their fa-

A Greater Appreciation for Freedom

The individuals who languished in prison camps during the war learned many truths about themselves and their nation. One of the most beneficial was to cherish those items which most take for granted. In the book *Three Came Home*, one prisoner, Agnes Keith, mentioned the lessons learned from captivity. The thoughts could have been expressed by any American soldier.

This is what freedom means to me. The right to live with, to touch and to love, my [spouse] and my children. The right to look about me without fear of seeing people beaten. The capacity to work for ourselves and our children.

The possession of a door, and a key with which to lock it. Moments of silence. A place in which to weep, with no one to see me doing so.

The freedom of my eyes to scan the face of the earth, the mountains, trees, fields, and sea, without barbed wire across my vision. The freedom of my body to walk with

the wind, and no sentry to stop me. Opportunity to earn the food to keep me strong. The ability to look each month at a new moon without asking, "How many more times must this beauty shine on my captivity?"

Those who lived through the Death March and captivity gained a greater awareness of what it meant to be free.

ther has an obsessive concern for the cleanliness and availability of food, for example, and why he plans against so many uncertainties." [130]

Forrest Knox has difficulty being around animals because he recalls the wild dogs at Cabanatuan that dug up shallow graves to eat the bodies of his dead comrades. "To this day I hate dogs with a passion. My children have dogs, but it was almost a personal insult if they brought them into the house and then expected me to play with them." [131]

Even though World War II ex-prisoners of war experienced numerous problems, most also claim they received some benefits. Though they would never hope to relive the war years, in some ways they became better people.

Clifford Fox said that being a prisoner made it

easier for me to accept setbacks because I've seen so many people who could not handle adversity. It also changed my attitude about people. We Americans tend to think we're the greatest, but there are great people all over the world. So being a POW made me more tolerant of others. It also made me more appreciative of what I have. [132]

Another boasted, "Afterwards you felt nothing was impossible. Whatever it was, you could do it, and you never allowed yourself to be bored again." [133]

Every man who endured time in a prisoner-of-war camp—whether it was for one month or as long as four years—had his life changed by the experience. Some suffered a great deal; others found an inner strength which they never knew existed. But all were affected.

More than half a century later, they still admit to the war's impact. "I will never be free of those prison years," [134] wrote one former prisoner of the Japanese.

★ Notes ★

Introduction: "I Just Tried to Forget Everything"

1. Quoted in Mark Jurkowitz, "Prisoners' Images Put a Face on American Role," *The Boston Globe*, April 2, 1999, p. 1.
2. Quoted in Linda R. Monk, ed., *Ordinary Americans*. Alexandria, VA: Close Up Publishing, 1994, p. 278.
3. Quoted in Lewis H. Carlson, *We Were Each Other's Prisoners: An Oral History of World War II American and German Prisoners of War*. New York: Basic Books, 1997, p. 116.

Chapter 1: "You Sure Don't Want to Die"

4. Quoted in Ronald H. Bailey, *Prisoners of War*. Alexandria, VA: Time-Life Books, 1981, p. 8.
5. Quoted in Bailey, *Prisoners of War*, p. 9.
6. John Mahoney, interview by author, February 23, 1992, Canton, Ohio.
7. Quoted in Meirion and Susie Harries, *Soldiers of the Sun: The Rise and Fall of the Imperial Japanese Army*. New York: Random House, 1991, p. 25.
8. Quoted in E. Bartlett Kerr, *Surrender and Survival: The Experience of American POWs in the Pacific, 1941–1945*. New York: William Morrow, 1985, pp. 36–37.
9. Quoted in Donald T. Giles Jr., ed., *Captive of the Rising Sun: The POW Memoirs of Rear Admiral Donald T. Giles, USN*. Annapolis, MD: Naval Institute Press, 1994, pp. 38, 42.
10. Quoted in Giles, *Captive of the Rising Sun*, p. 48.
11. Quoted in Giles, *Captive of the Rising Sun*, p. xiii.
12. Quoted in Harry Spiller, ed., *Prisoners of Nazis: Accounts by American POWs in World War II*. Jefferson, NC: McFarland Company, Inc., 1998, p. 27.
13. Quoted in Spiller, *Prisoners of Nazis*, p. 45.
14. Quoted in Spiller, *Prisoners of Nazis*, p. 56.

Chapter 2: "Guests for an Indefinite Stay"

15. Quoted in John C. McManus, *The Deadly Brotherhood: The American Combat Soldier in World War II*. Novato, CA: Presidio Press, 1998, p. 193.
16. Quoted in Robert Leckie, *Delivered From Evil: The Saga of World War II*. New York: Harper and Row, 1987, p. 811.
17. Quoted in Carlson, *We Were Each Other's Prisoners*, p. 48.

18. John A. Vietor, *Time Out: American Airmen at Stalag Luft I*. New York: Richard R. Smith, 1951, pp. 27–28.
19. Quoted in Carlson, *We Were Each Other's Prisoners*, p. 9.
20. Giles, *Captive of the Rising Sun*, p. 50.
21. Giles, *Captive of the Rising Sun*, p. 43.
22. Vietor, *Time Out*, p. 21.
23. Giles, *Captive of the Rising Sun*, p. 61.
24. William Nolan, interview by author, April 20, 1991.
25. Quoted in Donald Knox, *Death March: The Survivors of Bataan*. San Diego: Harcourt Brace Jovanovich, 1981, p. 121.
26. William Nolan, interview by author, April 20, 1991.
27. Quoted in Knox, *Death March*, p. 146.
28. Joseph Kutch, interview by author, April 25, 1991.
29. Quoted in Knox, *Death March*, p. 203.
30. William Nolan, interview by author, April 20, 1991.
31. Joseph Kutch, interview by author, April 25, 1991.
32. Vietor, *Time Out*, pp. 43–44.
33. Giles, *Captive of the Rising Sun*, p. 77.

Chapter 3: "Home Away from Home"

34. Vietor, *Time Out*, p. 62.
35. Giles, *Captive of the Rising Sun*, p. 74.
36. Giles, *Captive of the Rising Sun*, p. 74.
37. Chaim Nussbaum, *Chaplain on the River Kwai: Story of a Prisoner of War*. New York: Shapolsky, 1988, p. 145.
38. Vietor, *Time Out*, p. 47.
39. Quoted in Bailey, *Prisoners of War*, p. 58.
40. Vietor, *Time Out*, pp. 117–18.
41. Giles, *Captive of the Rising Sun*, p. 85.
42. Vietor, *Time Out*, p. 126.
43. Giles, *Captive of the Rising Sun*, pp. 121–22.
44. Quoted in Spiller, *Prisoners of the Nazis*, p. 17.
45. Quoted in Spiller, *Prisoners of the Nazis*, p. 16.
46. Giles, *Captive of the Rising Sun*, p. 154.
47. Quoted in Knox, *Death March*, p. 211.

Chapter 4: "Would Things Ever Get Better?"

48. Giles, *Captive of the Rising Sun*, p. 99.
49. Giles, *Captive of the Rising Sun*, p. 99.
50. Quoted in Knox, *Death March*, p. 260.
51. William E. Dyess, *The Dyess Story*. New York: G. P. Putnam's Sons, 1944, pp. 112–13.
52. Quoted in Carlson, *We Were Each Other's Prisoners*, p. 73.
53. Vietor, *Time Out*, p. 56.
54. Quoted in Carlson, *We Were Each Other's Prisoners*, p. vii.
55. Vietor, *Time Out*, p. 141.
56. Giles, *Captive of the Rising Sun*, p. 103.
57. Quoted in Spiller, *Prisoners of Nazis*, p. 146.
58. Giles, *Captive of the Rising Sun*, p. 134.
59. Vietor, *Time Out*, pp. 66, 70.
60. Giles, *Captive of the Rising Sun*, p. 131.
61. Quoted in Carlson, *We Were Each Other's Prisoners*, pp. 130–31.
62. Quoted in Carlson, *We Were Each Other's Prisoners*, p. 134.

Chapter 5: "A War of Wills"

63. Quoted in Bailey, *Prisoners of War*, p. 25.
64. Giles, *Captive of the Rising Sun*, p. 98.
65. Quoted in Knox, *Death March*, p. 236.
66. Quoted in Ernest Gordon, *Through the Valley of the Kwai*. New York: Harper and Row, 1962, p. 3.
67. Quoted in Knox, *Death March*, p. 420.
68. Quoted in Knox, *Death March*, p. 433.
69. Vietor, *Time Out*, p. 94.
70. Giles, *Captive of the Rising Sun*, p. 80.
71. Quoted in Carlson, *We Were Each Other's Prisoners*, p. 71.
72. Vietor, *Time Out*, p. 27.
73. Quoted in Knox, *Death March*, p. 240.
74. Vietor, *Time Out*, p. 145.
75. Giles, *Captive of the Rising Sun*, p. 55.
76. Vietor, *Time Out*, p. 143.
77. Quoted in Carlson, *We Were Each Other's Prisoners*, p. 79.
78. Quoted in Carlson, *We Were Each Other's Prisoners*, p. 72.
79. Giles, *Captive of the Rising Sun*, p. 123.
80. Quoted in Carlson, *We Were Each Other's Prisoners*, pp. 81–82.
81. Ralph Holewinski, interview by author, October 12, 1988, Romulus, Michigan.
82. Quoted in Knox, *Death March*, p. 242.
83. Quoted in Knox, *Death March*, p. 345.
84. Nolan, Interview.
85. Vietor, *Time Out*, p. 60.

Chapter 6: "We Are Free!"

86. Giles, *Captive of the Rising Sun*, pp. 129–30.
87. Agnes Newton Keith, *Three Came Home.* Boston: Little, Brown, 1947, p. 241.
88. Quoted in Carlson, *We Were Each Other's Prisoners*, pp. 84–85.
89. Quoted in Carlson, *We Were Each Other's Prisoners*, p. 119.
90. Giles, *Captive of the Rising Sun*, p. 144.
91. Nussbaum, *Chaplain on the River Kwai*, p. 253.
92. Quoted in Bailey, *Prisoners of War*, p. 171.
93. Quoted in Giles, *Captive of the Rising Sun*, p. 154.
94. Quoted in Knox, *Death March*, pp. 340, 343.
95. Quoted in Knox, *Death March*, p. 342.
96. Quoted in Knox, *Death March*, p. 350.
97. Quoted in Bailey, *Prisoners of War*, p. 186.
98. Quoted in Carlson, *We Were Each Other's Prisoners*, p. 15.
99. Nussbaum, *Chaplain on the River Kwai*, p. 254.
100. Quoted in Kerr, *Surrender and Survival*, p. 280.
101. Quoted in Christopher Cross, *Soldiers of God.* New York: E. P. Dutton, 1945, p. 58.
102. Nussbaum, *Chaplain on the River Kwai*, p. 255.

Chapter 7: "I Will Never Be Free of Those Prison Years"

103. Quoted in Carlson, *We Were Each Other's Prisoners*, p. 85.
104. Quoted in Bailey, *Prisoners of War*, p. 176.
105. Giles, *Captive of the Rising Sun*, p. 160.

106. Giles, *Captive of the Rising Sun*, p. 162.

107. Giles, *Captive of the Rising Sun*, p. 162.

108. Quoted in Knox, *Death March*, p. 452.

109. Giles, *Captive of the Rising Sun*, pp. 165–66.

110. Giles, *Captive of the Rising Sun*, p. 171.

111. Vietor, *Time Out*, p. 192.

112. Quoted in Spiller, *Prisoners of Nazis*, p. 54.

113. Giles, *Captive of the Rising Sun*, p. 172.

114. Quoted in Carlson, *We Were Each Other's Prisoners*, p. 90.

115. Giles, *Captive of the Rising Sun*, p. xiii.

116. Quoted in Carlson, *We Were Each Other's Prisoners*, p. 116.

117. Quoted in Knox, *Death March*, pp. 461–62.

118. Quoted in Carlson, *We Were Each Other's Prisoners*, p. 231.

119. Quoted in Carlson, *We Were Each Other's Prisoners*, p. 232.

120. Quoted in Carlson, *We Were Each Other's Prisoners*, p. 249.

121. Giles, *Captive of the Rising Sun*, pp. 173–74.

122. Quoted in Giles, *Captive of the Rising Sun*, p. 181.

123. Quoted in Knox, *Death March*, p. 475.

124. Quoted in Knox, *Death March*, p. 478.

125. Quoted in Carlson, *We Were Each Other's Prisoners*, p. 239.

126. Quoted in Carlson, *We Were Each Other's Prisoners*, p. 225.

127. Quoted in Knox, *Death March*, pp. 476–77.

128. Quoted in Carlson, *We Were Each Other's Prisoners*, p. 183.

129. Quoted in Carlson, *We Were Each Other's Prisoners*, pp. 248–49.

130. Robert E. Haney, *Caged Dragons: An American P.O.W. in WWII Japan*. Ann Arbor, MI: Sabre Press, 1991, p. 261.

131. Quoted in Knox, *Death March*, p. 225.

132. Quoted in Carlson, *We Were Each Other's Prisoners*, p. 249.

133. Quoted in Carlson, *We Were Each Other's Prisoners*, p. xxv.

134. Keith, *Three Came Home*, p. 310.

★ Chronology of Events ★

1929

Representatives from more than forty nations sign the Geneva Convention.

1941

December 7–8: The first American prisoners are taken captive when Japan strikes throughout the Pacific; Guam falls; Wake Island falls.

1942

April: Bataan falls and the Death March begins.

May: Corregidor falls; the Japanese prime minister announces a policy for prisoners of "no work, no food"; invasion of North Africa produces the first large group of American POWs in the war against Germany.

1943

William E. Dyess escapes from a Japanese camp and brings word of the Bataan Death March to the United States; invasion of Italy produces another large group of prisoners in Europe.

1944

March 24: The "Great Escape" from Stalag Luft III occurs.

June 6: D day brings Allied forces to the European mainland and produces another large group of prisoners.

September–December: Japan transports American prisoners to Japan on the infamous "Hell Ships."

December: The Battle of the Bulge yields the final large group of prisoners in Europe.

1945

Many American prisoners endure forced marches to other camps; American, British, and Russian forces begin liberating prisoners confined in German camps; former prisoners of war return to the United States.

May 8: The war in Europe ends.

August 6 and 8: Atom bombs are dropped on Japan.

August 15: The war in the Pacific ends.

1949

The U.S. government agrees to pay ex-prisoners of war two dollars for each day they were confined.

1985

The U.S. Congress creates the Prisoner of War Medal.

⭐ **For Further Reading** ⭐

June A. English and Thomas D. Jones, *Scholastic Encyclopedia of the United States at War.* New York: Scholastic, 1998. This work provides a helpful summary of every major action involving the United States.

William W. Lace, *The Holocaust Library: The Nazis.* San Diego: Lucent Books, 1998. The author delivers a comprehensive overview of life under Adolf Hitler's Nazi rule.

R. Conrad Stein, *World War II in Europe.* Springfield, NJ: Enslow, 1994. A summary of events in Europe during the war.

———, *World War II in the Pacific.* Springfield, NJ: Enslow, 1994. A companion volume to Stein's book on the European theater.

Gail B. Stewart, *Hitler's Reich.* San Diego: Lucent Books, 1994. Another useful look at life in Germany during the war years.

Helen Strahinich, *The Holocaust: Understanding and Remembering.* Springfield, NJ: Enslow, 1996. The book's presentation of life in concentration camps gives an idea of conditions which existed for prisoners of war, although they were not as horrendous for the Americans as they were for Jewish inmates.

☆ Works Consulted ☆

Ronald H. Bailey, *Prisoners of War*. Alexandria, VA: Time-Life Books, 1981. This superb examination of prisoners of war in both theaters contains fluid writing and numerous excellent photographs.

Lewis H. Carlson, *We Were Each Other's Prisoners: An Oral History of World War II American and German Prisoners of War*. New York: Basic Books, 1997. Relying mainly on interviews with former American and German prisoners of war, Carlson constructs an informative account of what life was like behind enemy barbed wire.

Haruko Taya Cook and Theodore F. Cook, *Japan at War: An Oral History*. New York: The New Press, 1992. Based upon interviews with Japanese soldiers and civilians, the authors present a fascinating glimpse of war from the Japanese point of view.

Christopher Cross, *Soldiers of God*. New York: E. P. Dutton, 1945. This book focuses on chaplains in service and includes a chapter describing time in prison camps.

William E. Dyess, *The Dyess Story*. New York: G. P. Putnam's Sons, 1944. This account, written by one of the first prisoners of war to escape a Japanese camp and return to American forces, stunned the nation when it appeared in 1944. Its graphic account of the Death March and atrocious conditions in prison camp, the first time that most civilians had heard of such things, solidified hatred of the enemy.

Editors of Time-Life Books, *Japan at War*. Alexandria, VA: Time-Life Books, 1980. A survey of life in Japan during the war, including some material on American prisoners. This is helpful for understanding Japanese attitudes toward POWs and why so little food was available.

Donald T. Giles Jr., ed., *Captive of the Rising Sun: The POW Memoirs of Rear Admiral Donald T. Giles, USN*. Annapolis, MD: Naval Institute Press, 1994. An outstanding account of a naval officer's time in Japanese prison camps, from his incarceration in the war's early days to the conflict's end. Giles imparts a tender, riveting account of life as a POW.

Ernest Gordon, *Through the Valley of the Kwai*. New York: Harper and Row, 1962. A beautifully written narrative of his time in Japanese prison camps in Burma. This book contains much helpful information.

Robert Guillain, *I Saw Tokyo Burning*. Garden City, NY: Doubleday, 1981. Written by a French journalist who spent the war years as a correspondent in Tokyo, this book contains much useful information on the Japanese attitude toward American prisoners of war.

Robert E. Haney, *Caged Dragons: An American P.O.W. in WWII Japan*. Ann Arbor, MI: Sabre Press, 1991. The author writes of his prison camp experiences with emotion and sometimes with anger. He is especially hard hitting on what he considers shoddy government treatment of ex-POWs after the war.

Meirion and Susie Harries, *Soldiers of the Sun: The Rise and Fall of the Imperial Japanese Army*. New York: Random House, 1991. A helpful study of the Japanese army and its attitudes toward fighting and prisoners.

Mark Jurkowitz, "Prisoners' Images Put a Face on American Role," *The Boston Globe*, April 2, 1999, p. 1.

Agnes Newton Keith, *Three Came Home*. Boston: Little, Brown, 1947. A classic account written by an American woman who spent more than three years in prison camps. This powerful book provides a fascinating glimpse at life behind barbed wire.

E. Bartlett Kerr, *Surrender and Survival: The Experience of American POWs in the Pacific, 1941–1945*. New York: William Morrow, 1985. An indispensable examination of the plight of POWs in Japanese prison camps, largely based on research and complemented with interviews with ex-POWs.

Donald Knox, *Death March: The Survivors of Bataan*. San Diego: Harcourt Brace Jovanovich, 1981. Based upon his interviews with survivors, the author delivers one of the most chilling accounts of life as a prisoner of the Japanese. While some narratives contain grisly detail, the reader will emerge with a deeper understanding of what made men act the way they did, how they survived, and why some bitterness remains so long after the war.

Robert Leckie, *Delivered From Evil: The Saga of World War II*. New York: Harper and Row, 1987. A one-volume history of World War II, written by a former marine who fought in the Pacific.

John C. McManus, *The Deadly Brotherhood: The American Combat Soldier in World War II*. Novato, CA: Presidio Press, 1998. A superb glimpse at life for American fighting men during World War II.

Linda R. Monk, ed., *Ordinary Americans*. Alexandria, VA: Close Up Publishing, 1994. A helpful compilation of narratives written by people who were present at various events in U.S. history.

Chaim Nussbaum, *Chaplain on the River Kwai: Story of a Prisoner of War*. New York: Shapolsky, 1988. Based upon a diary kept by Rabbi Nussbaum, this book contains vivid descriptions of camp life and conveys the emotional and spiritual trauma experienced by prisoners. Numerous sketches, drawn by a prisoner, add to the book's value.

Duane Schultz, *Hero of Bataan: The Story of General Jonathan M. Wainwright*. New York: St. Martin's Press, 1981. The biography of the highest-ranking American prisoner of war includes many useful comments about conditions for prisoners and about their hopes, dreams, and frustrations.

Harry Spiller, ed., *Prisoners of Nazis: Accounts by American POWs in World War II.* Jefferson, NC: McFarland & Company, Inc., 1998. A compilation of interviews with ex-prisoners of war that provide a superb image of life in German prison camps.

John Toland, *But Not In Shame.* New York: Random House, 1961. A noted historian examines the war's first six months in this readable, compelling volume.

John A. Vietor, *Time Out: American Airmen at Stalag Luft I.* New York: Richard R. Smith, 1951. Written by a prisoner of war, the book provides a comprehensive look at what life was like in a German prisoner-of-war camp.

Keith Wheeler, *The Fall of Japan.* Alexandria, VA: Time-Life Books, 1983. A study of conditions in Japan as the war wound down, with some emphasis on the plight of prisoners in the final harrowing days.

✯ **Index** ✯

★ Picture Credits ★

Cover Photo: Corbis
American Stock/Archive Photos, 72, 80
AP/Wide World Photos, 7 (top), 9, 10, 36 (right), 41, 51, 53,
    60, 63, 84, 85, 86, 94
Archive Photos, 35, 36 (left),48, 54, 61, 69, 74, 79
Corbis, 5, 19, 26, 27, 43, 49, 71, 73, 77, 81, 88, 90, 96
Corbis/AFP, 7 (bottom)
Corbis/Hulton-Deutsch Collection, 38, 66, 75
Corbis/Ira Nowinski, 28
Corbis/Joseph Schwartz Collection, 14
Corbis-Bettmann, 12, 13, 17, 21, 22, 30, 31, 33, 39, 67
Digital Stock, 11, 20, 46, 47, 55
John W. Mahoney, 23
Paramount Studios/Archive Photos, 45
pixelpartners, 62
United Artists/Archive Photos, 58, 92

☆ About the Author ☆

John F. Wukovits is a junior high school teacher and writer from Trenton, Michigan, who specializes in history and biography. Besides biographies of Anne Frank, Jim Carrey, Stephen King, and Martin Luther King Jr. for Lucent, he has written biographies of the World War II commander Admiral Clifton Sprague, Barry Sanders, Tim Allen, Jack Nicklaus, Vince Lombardi, and Wyatt Earp. A graduate of the University of Notre Dame, Wukovits is the father of three daughters—Amy, Julie, and Karen.